WRITERS AND THEIR WORK

ISOBEL ARMSTRONG
General Editor

BRYAN LOUGHREY
Advisory Editor

W. H. Auden

© Copyright 1997 by Stan Smith

First published in 1997 by Northcote House Publishers Ltd, Plymbridge House,
Estover Road, Plymouth PL6 7PY, United Kingdom.
Tel: +44 (0) 1752 202368. Fax: +44 (0) 1752 202330.

British Library Cataloguing-in-Publication Data
A catalogue record for this book is available from the British Library

ISBN 0 7463 0736 5

Typeset by PDQ Typesetting, Newcastle-under-Lyme
Printed and bound in the United Kingdom

For Edith Smith

born the same day as Auden, still going strong
'She *is* our Mum'

Contents

Acknowledgements

I would like to thank the University of Dundee for study leave to complete this project. Auden and Auden studies are fortunate in having in Edward Mendelson a dedicated and generous advocate, and I am personally grateful to him for much encouragement and many kindnesses over the years. Gwen Hunter and Ann Bain and my colleague on the Auden Concordance Project, Rob Watt, have been unstinting in their support. Hilary Walford was an excellent copy-editor. Philip Smith helped in innumerable ways. As always my love and thanks to Jennifer Birkett for being there. Finally, my publishers and I are grateful to the Estate of W. H. Auden, Faber & Faber Ltd. in England and Random House Inc. in the USA for permission to quote from the works of W. H. Auden.

Biographical Outline

1907	21 February: born at York, third son of George Augustus and Constance Rosalie Bicknell Auden.
1908	Family moves to Birmingham; father appointed Chief Medical Officer for Schools and Professor of Public Health at the University.
1914–18	First World War ('Father at the wars').
1915	Boarder at St Edmund's preparatory school, Hindhead, Surrey, where he meets Christopher Isherwood, a fellow pupil.
1917	Russian Revolution.
1920–5	Boarder at Gresham's School, Holt. Reads Freud. Falls in love with Robert Medley, a fellow pupil, who suggests he write poetry. First poem published in school magazine.
1925	Visits Europe with his father, staying in Kitzbühel, Austria, with his father's friend Frau Hedwig Petzold.
1925–8	Exhibitioner at Christ Church, Oxford, studying Natural Sciences, then PPE, and finally English; graduates with a Third.
1926	General Strike. Meets Tom Driberg; reads Eliot's *The Waste Land*. Revisits Austria, where has first heterosexual experience with Frau Petzold, some years older than him.
1928	Auden's *Poems* published privately by Stephen Spender. August: begins a year in Berlin; encounters left-wing politics.
1929	In Berlin, involved by John Layard in his bungled suicide attempt. Returns from Germany; teaches in

	London. October: Wall Street Crash inaugurates the Depression years.
1930–2	Teacher at the Larchfield School, Helensburgh, where he writes *The Orators*. T. S. Eliot arranges publication of 'Paid on Both Sides' in his journal *The Criterion*, and of *Poems* with Faber & Faber.
1932–5	Teacher at Downs School, Colwall, Malvern.
1933	Hitler elected German Reichskanzler. *The Dance of Death* published (performed by the Group Theatre 1934).
1935	Marries Erika Mann to provide her with a passport to leave Germany. Works for GPO Film Unit.
1935–8	Writes, with Isherwood, three plays: *The Dog Beneath the Skin* (1935); *The Ascent of F6* (1936); *On the Frontier* (1938); all produced by the Group Theatre.
1936	*Look Stranger!* published (as *On This Island*, New York, 1937). With Louis MacNeice visits Iceland (joint work, *Letters from Iceland*, published 1937). Spanish Civil War begins with Franco's insurrection (ends with Republic's defeat, 1939).
1937	January–March: in Spain, broadcasts for Republic; publishes *Spain*. Meets Charles Williams. Teaches at Downs School.
1938	With Isherwood visits a war-torn China, returning via Japan and USA (joint work, *Journey to a War*, published 1939). March, German *Anschluss* with Austria. September, Chamberlain's Munich Agreement cedes Czech Sudetenland to Hitler.
1939	January: leaves Britain for USA; lives in Brooklyn Heights, New York, until 1941. March, Hitler occupies Prague. April, Auden meets Chester Kallman, an 18-year old blond student. August, Nazi–Soviet Pact. 1 September: Hitler invades Poland; 3 September: Britain and France declare war.
1940	Publishes *Another Time*. Teaches at New School for Social Research, New York. Meets Niebuhrs; rediscovers Christianity.
1941	Publishes *The Double Man* in USA (*New Year Letter* in UK). Benjamin Britten's operetta *Paul Bunyan* (libretto by Auden) performed at Columbia Univer-

	sity. Teaches at Olivet College, Michigan, and Michigan University, Ann Arbor.
1942–5	Teaches at Swarthmore and Bryn Mawr Colleges.
1944	*For the Time Being*, published in the USA. Meets Rhoda Jaffe, with whom he has an intermittent affair between 1945 and 1948.
1945	War ends with the atom-bombing of Japan. Returns to Europe as major in US Airforce Strategic Bombing Survey, with the commission to monitor effects of civilian bombing and contact anti-Nazis. Visits UK. Moves to New York. *The Collected Poetry* published in USA.
1946	Becomes US citizen. Teaches at Bennington College and New School for Social Research. Prolonged affair with Rhoda Jaffe.
1947	Teaches religion at Barnard College. *The Age of Anxiety*.
1949	Page-Barbour Lectures at University of Virginia (published as *The Enchafèd Flood*, 1950).
1949–57	Spring/summer: rents house on Ischia, island near Capri.
1950	*Collected Shorter Poems 1939–1944* published in UK. Teaches at Mount Holyoke College. Korean War starts.
1951	Soviet spy Guy Burgess seeks to use Auden's Ischian house in process of defecting. *Nones* published in the USA; Stravinsky's *The Rake's Progress* (libretto by Auden and Kallman) performed in Venice.
1953–72	House at 77 St Mark's Place, New York; Research Professor, Smith College.
1955	*The Shield of Achilles*.
1956–61	Professor of Poetry, Oxford University.
1958	With proceeds of an Italian literary prize, buys farmhouse in the village of Kirchstetten, Lower Austria, which he shares with Kallman until his death (in later years Kallman spends much of his time in Athens, with a series of Evzones).
1960	*Homage to Clio*.
1961	Hans Werner Henze's *Elegy for Young Lovers* (libretto by Auden and Kallman) performed in Stuttgart.

1962	*The Dyer's Hand* published in USA.
1964	Revisits Iceland; spends six months on Ford Foundation artists-in-residence programme in Berlin.
1965	*About the House* published in the USA.
1966	Henze's *The Bassarids* (libretto by Auden and Kallman) performed in Salzburg. *Collected Shorter Poems.*
1968	*Collected Longer Poems* and *Secondary Worlds.*
1969	*City Without Walls.*
1970	*A Certain World* published in USA.
1971	*Academic Graffiti.*
1972	While staying at All Souls, Oxford, is robbed by a young labourer. Lives in the grounds of Christ Church, Oxford. Publishes *Epistle to a Godson* (for Spender's nephew Philip).
1973	Nicholas Nabokov's *Love's Labours Lost* (libretto by Auden and Kallman) performed in Brussels. *Forewords and Afterwords* published. 29 September: after delivering a talk in Vienna, dies of heart attack in a small hotel in the Walfischgasse, close to the Staatsoper. Buried in the Kirchstetten churchyard.
1974	*Thank You, Fog.*
1975	January: Kallman dies in Athens, aged 54.

Abbreviations and References

Auden periodically revised and sometimes excised whole poems from his work. Unless otherwise indicated, all poetry references are to first publication in volume form, published by Faber & Faber in the UK and Random House in the USA. Auden's final versions can be found in the *Collected Poems* (1976; new edn. 1991), the original versions of 1930s writings in *The English Auden*, and a variety of both in *Selected Poems* (all edited by Edward Mendelson). For fuller details, see the Select Bibliography. Where possible, reference to the prose is to first separate publication. For the reader's convenience, page references to the prose collections, where appropriate, are added to endnotes, and throughout the text, using the following abbreviations.

DH   *The Dyer's Hand and Other Essays* (new edn., London: Faber & Faber; New York: Random House, 1975)

EA   *The English Auden: Poems, Essays and Dramatic Writings, 1927–1939*, ed. Edward Mendelson (London: Faber & Faber; New York: Random House, 1977)

FA   *Forewords and Afterwords*, ed. Edward Mendelson (new edn., London: Faber & Faber; New York: Random House, 1979)

1

We are Lived by Powers

THE VIEW FROM BIRMINGHAM

W. H. Auden has been described as 'the first poet writing in English who felt at home in the twentieth century'.[1] Certainly he is the only poet to have given his name decisively to a key epoch of that century. Despite recent revisionist attempts to rewrite the 1930s, its writers are likely to remain 'the Auden Generation',[2] and the era to retain his characterization of it in 'September 1, 1939' as 'a low dishonest decade'.

The autobiographical light verse of 'Letter to Lord Byron', a major sequence in *Letters from Iceland* (1937), states clearly what it was that Auden found so homely about the century:

> Tramlines and slagheaps, pieces of machinery,
> That was, and still is, my ideal scenery.

In a nose-thumbing gesture to Wordsworthian nature mysticism, the poem also celebrated the industrial landscapes of the West Midlands in which Auden grew up, asserting that

> Clearer than Scafell Pike, my heart has stamped on
> The view from Birmingham to Wolverhampton.

The poem hails with heavy irony the 'New World' of those who love 'antiseptic objects', and 'feel at home' with Lewis Mumford's futuristic utopia of national electricity grids (a new thing in the 1930s), alloys, plate glass, chromium furniture, and Aertex underwear for boys. Auden makes clear his contempt for all these; the last seems to have a particular resonance. Throughout his life Auden saw hygiene as a repressive and faddish modern neurosis and distrusted the squeaky clean and the politically correct. In serio-comic defiance of what 'Letter to Lord Byron' calls the totalitarian 'Goddess of bossy underlings,

1

Normality... Reeking of antiseptics', he is reported never to have worn underpants, and the sympathy proclaimed in 'Prologue at Sixty' for the buttons, beards and Be-ins of the 1960s Hippy generation reaffirmed a lifelong if campishly distanced affinity with bohemia.

There was always an element of nostalgia, as of grime, to Auden's sense of homeliness. His ideal scenery is modern precisely in its outdatedness, a superseded order strangely surviving into the present, littered with the debris of 'slattern' tenements and run-down factories from an older world. True modernity means embracing the unlovely landscapes, the *paysages démoralisés*, left behind by the industrial revolution. One of his earliest poems, later called 'The Watershed', describes a landscape which, 'cut off, will not communicate', a marginal territory part-urban, part-rural, and dominated by 'An industry already comatose, | Yet sparsely living'. This world of dismantled washing-floors, ramshackle water pumps, flooded workings, damaged shafts, abandoned levels Auden was to make peculiarly his own. The danger scented in the poem's closing lines comes to one who is both inheritor and stranger in this landscape. 'Frustrate and vexed', he hesitates at a crux and watershed (points where destinies diverge), urged to go back but unable to return, suffering the anxiety of the threshold, always about to begin, but as in a nightmare paralysed, unable to start out.

The prevailing mood of these poems has its origins in a public history inseparable from a personal state of mind. The same primal landscape recurs, its significance indicated by the opening symbol of the beautiful sestina, 'Hearing of harvests rotting in the valleys'. These poems are full of the sense of a possible plenty destroyed by outrageous neglect, and of the vexed frustration of the new young self who wants to do something about it all, but meets resistance or indifference from his seniors, as in the memorable, robust rhythms, mocking Tennyson's 'Locksley Hall', of 'Get there if you can':

Get there if you can and see the land you once were proud to own
Though the roads have almost vanished and the expresses never run:
Smokeless chimneys, damaged bridges, rotting wharves and choked
    canals,
Tramlines buckled, smashed trucks lying on their side across the rails.

Wystan Hugh Auden was born on 21 February 1907 in York, the third and last son of a doctor and a nurse. His family moved when he was a year old to Birmingham, where his father became Chief Medical Officer for Schools and later Professor of Public Health at the University. Auden came to consciousness in a secure upper-middle-class world at a time when, as he wrote nostalgically in 1964 in 'The Cave of Making', railway engines were named after Arthurian knights, science was known to schoolboys as 'stinks', and 'the Manor was still politically numinous'. Since then, the churches have emptied, the cavalry disappeared, and 'any faith, if we had it, in immanent virtue died'. What he figures here is a predicament that links early and late Auden: the sense of human society and of the individual self as moulded by economic and historical forces which orchestrate their very being, and the contrary impulsion of classes and individuals to understand and, in the process, transcend those circumstances, finding an existential freedom in the recognition of necessity.

The great modern systems of thought by which Auden sought to understand himself and his age all had roots in the nineteenth century. Indeed, in *New Year Letter* (published as *The Double Man* in the USA), the long discursive poem which in 1941 confirmed his American expatriation, he spoke of them as systems which brought a whole epoch of intellectual enquiry to its close: Charles Darwin's theory of evolution, Karl Marx's exposure of what Auden's 1933 play *The Dance of Death* called 'the economic | Reasons for our acts', and Sigmund Freud's account of the unconscious which, though largely adumbrated in this century, had its origins in the preoccupations of *fin-de-siècle* Vienna. Even Auden's return to Christianity in the 1940s drew its strength from the thought of the nineteenth-century existentialist philosopher Søren Kierkegaard. What linked all these systems for Auden was an interpretation of identity as at once shaped by and in conflict with the material and social conditions to which it was born.

A 1939 essay spelt out his conviction that Marxist thought simply extended Darwinian ideas into the socio-economic sphere:

> The history of life on this planet is the history of the ways in which life has gained control over and freedom within its environ-

ment.... Below the human level, this progress has taken place through structural biological changes, depending on the luck of mutations or the chances of natural selection. Only man, with his conscious intelligence, has been able to continue his evolution after his biological development has finished. By studying the laws of physical nature, he has gained a large measure of control over them and insofar as he is able to understand the laws of his own nature and of the societies in which he lives, he approaches that state where what he wills may be done. 'Freedom', as a famous definition has it, 'is consciousness of necessity.'[3]

'We live in freedom of necessity', he wrote more poetically in *Journey to a War* the same year, 'A mountain people living among mountains'. The sonnet sequence from which this comes, 'In Time of War', traces in mythic form the whole evolution of the human species, journeying not only towards the next world war but also, as Auden then saw it, towards that final struggle which would free human life from the constraints of ignorance and benighted social organization. As this sequence implies and *New Year Letter* was to argue forcibly, Kierkegaard's emphasis on individual responsibility complemented Marxism for Auden with a vision of the subject's lonely freedom at the interface of social, biological and psychological necessities.

Auden's 1939 essay spells out his conviction that 'Man has always been a social animal living in communities': 'The individual *in vacuo* is an intellectual abstraction. The individual is the product of social life', without which it would be no more than 'a bundle of unconditioned reflexes'. Marx was 'correct in his view that physical conditions and the forms of economic production have dictated the forms of communities', so that, for example, the mountainous geography of ancient Greece 'produced small democratic city-states, while the civilisations based on river irrigation like Egypt and Mesopotamia were centralised autocratic empires'. As individuals we are 'each conscious of ourselves as a thinking, feeling, and willing whole', with a sense of selfhood and independent choice, but we can exercise this properly only when we understand the social forces which shape us. Anthropologists such as Ruth Benedict and the Lynds, studying respectively primitive American culture and contemporary middle America, have revealed 'the enormous power of a given cultural form to determine the nature of the

4

individuals who live under it', for every culture fosters those character traits and behavioural modes most useful to it (*EA* 373). To such studies Auden added elsewhere the work on Melanesia of Malinowski and his own mentor, John Layard. In 1931–2 he drew on Layard's account of the Flying Tricksters of Malekula for a methodology with which to explain the mysteries of contemporary Britain in his 'English Study', *The Orators*. For Auden, then, understanding himself meant studying the discourses of Englishness which had shaped him.

WHO AM I NOW?

If material circumstances determine identity, their most crucial mediation for Auden was the profoundly social medium of a national language, which tells us not only *what* but *how* to think, feel, know, shaping the very foundations of the self. 'England to me is my own tongue, | And what I did when I was young', he wrote in American retrospect in *New Year Letter*. But if language constructs identity, it also offers the tools for understanding which enable us to rise above such constructions. A 1948 essay, 'The Greeks and Us', extended the argument of *I Believe* by claiming that Greek geography had fostered a civilization based on diversity, migration and an economy of exchange, and thus stimulated an intellectual climate of 'comprehension, inquiry, speculation, and experiment'. The great achievement of the Greeks was to teach us 'to think about our thinking', to 'look at [our] self and [our] world as if they were not [ours] but a stranger's'.[4]

The title of Auden's 1936 collection, *Look, Stranger!*, had announced this theme a decade earlier (though Auden himself preferred the American title *On This Island*). The poem which provides both titles invites us to look with a stranger's eye on contemporary Britain, 'this island now'. There is a sense of passionate urgency to that adverb which, a year later, was explained in the famous phrase of the pamphlet poem *Spain*, 'Yesterday all the past.... But to-day the struggle'. For Auden the self at any moment is always double, determined by its past, but capable of self-determination in the present, facing that existential choice in the 'now' of today ('I am your choice, your decision: yes, I am Spain') which can determine a future. The doubleness of *The Double Man* is explained in the book's epigraph from that perennial sceptic Montaigne: 'We are, I know not how, double in ourselves, so that what we believe we disbelieve, and cannot rid ourselves of what we condemn.'

It was a conviction only strengthened by Auden's wartime conversion back to an existentialist Christianity that stressed the responsibility of the individual freely to choose an absolute commitment, in which agonizing doubt is the very foundation of authentic belief. That moment of decision had already figured in *Spain* as the recognition of necessity, the international volunteers converging on war-ravaged Madrid 'to present their lives' and, in the process, help to build 'the Just City'. It remains the preoccupation of a post-war poem such as 'Memorial for the City' (1949) and is the presiding theme and ultimate aspiration of such late volumes as *City Without Walls* (1969).

In the epilogue to this book, ironically entitled 'Prologue at Sixty', the poet, by now an American citizen for two decades, asks disingenuously:

> Who am I now?
> An American? No, a New Yorker,
> who opens his *Times* at the obit page,
> whose dream images date him already.

'Who am I now?' is a rather different question from 'Who am I?', since it assumes a state of the self in which identity is not fixed and monolithic but fluid and changing, one in which the question itself may be an attempt to pin down something tenuous and transient at the very moment that it implies the danger and unreliability of any such fixing.

Auden's proviso in reply to questions about the Vietnam War around the same time might suggest that he is here thinking of the American, not the British, *Times*: 'it would be absurd to call this answer mine,' he noted. 'It simply means that I am an American citizen who reads *The New York Times*.'[5] So much of what one regards as one's own intellectual property, he implies, really depends on second-hand opinions superficially acquired. In fact, the poem's cultural allegiance hovers unresolved in mid-Atlantic. At a deeper level he remains an Englishman of the upper middle class, turning first, in an act specific to that class and culture, to the obituary columns of the London *Times* to see who among his Establishment contemporaries has died recently, and expecting to find in those exclusive columns people he knows personally. Identity is shaped by discourse at a level deeper than that of mere ideas, as the sly ambiguity of the word 'date' implies. Awake, he finds himself in the electronic era of lasers, computers, bugged telephones, and sophisticated weapon systems. But the imagery of his dreams calls up the world in which he was young, even its Freudian symbols deriving from an older technology of steam, coal, gas and water. These images 'date' him to a specific era, revealing his unconscious to be already dated. But they also 'date' him in the slangy American sense of the word first used with neophyte glee at his own up-to-dateness when, newly arrived in new York, he playfully put down his new American love with anecdotes of his first, English one, in the poem 'Heavy Date':

> Love requires an Object,
> But this varies so much,
> Almost, I imagine,
>   Anything will do:
> When I was a child, I
> Loved a pumping-engine,
> Thought it every bit as
>   Beautiful as you.

The subject finds itself in the nomination of its objects, in an arena supplied by history. In 'Prologue at Sixty', standing on the Austrian ground he has made his final home, he still finds his unconscious assumptions about what is 'natural' shaped by the libidinal landscapes of his first world, feeling the absence of hedgerows 'odd', though he knows well enough that this 'unenglish tract' simply reveals the historicity of his expectations. Hedgerows seem normal to him only because, in the eighteenth century, Whig landlords, in an act of economic class warfare, enclosed English common lands with privatizing hedgerows.

In this late poem, as in the politically committed works of the 1930s, power, class and all the tainted discourses of history are still seen to insert themselves into the most apparently innocent and spontaneous of perceptions. How they do this can be explained for Auden by that great liberator of consciousness,

Sigmund Freud, whose ideas are apparent in the playful use of psychoanalysis in 'Heavy Date'. In a powerful elegy in 1939 for his friend, the German left-wing poet and dramatist Ernst Toller, a refugee from Nazism who had committed suicide in New York shortly after Auden's arrival there, Auden speculated on the causes of his death, concluding

> We are lived by powers we pretend to understand:
> They arrange our loves; it is they who direct at the end
> The enemy bullet, the sickness, or even our hand.

If Toller died by his own hand, that hand was ultimately directed by external powers so deeply internalized as to be part of the very construction of the self. It may be, as 'In Memory of Ernst Toller' suggests, that Toller's suicide stemmed from something horrid the small child he once was saw in the woodshed long ago. The unexpectedly playful allusion is to Stella Gibbon's Aunt Ada Doom in her 1932 novel *Cold Comfort Farm*, whose tyranny over her family is wielded from the bedroom to which she retired years ago because as a girl she saw 'something nasty in the woodshed'. Toller's woodshed is that 'Europe which took refuge in [his] head', a Germany twenty years ago 'Already... too injured to get well', beset by military defeat, economic collapse and social anarchy, where, in a Munich prison cell, the young writer had faced execution for his part in the month-long Bavarian Soviet.

'September 1, 1939' develops the grim childish make-believe, speaking of those bewildered by the onset of the Second World War as children 'Lost in a haunted wood... | Who have never been happy or good'. Here Auden again speculates on the social causes of neurosis in the formation of the child, seeing Hitler's psychopathology as the product of 'the whole offence | From Luther until now | That has driven a culture mad'. If accurate scholarship might unlock these traumas, it is to Marx and Freud that the poet still looks for enlightenment. The differences between them as diagnosticians are simply ones of method, he had proposed in 'Psychology and Art To-day':

> Both Marx and Freud start from the failures of civilisation, one from the poor, one from the ill. Both see human behaviour determined, not consciously, but by instinctive needs, hunger and love. Both desire a world where rational choice and self-determination are

possible. The difference between them is the inevitable difference between the man who studies crowds in the street, and the man who sees the patient, or at most the family, in the consulting-room. Marx sees the direction of the relations between outer and inner world from without inwards, Freud vice versa.[6]

'In Memory of Sigmund Freud', Auden's elegy for 'an important Jew who died in exile' in the very month war broke out, was published along with the Toller poem, 'September 1, 1939', and an elegy for Auden's poetic father-figure W. B. Yeats in the same section of *Another Time* (1940), his first American collection. What the elegy calls the 'rational voice' of Freudian psychoanalysis had sought to understand the powers by which we are lived, seeking the unconscious origins of our behaviour in the repressions of infancy, so as to transform the 'delectable creatures' of the unconscious into allies rather than enemies, 'exiles who long for the future | that lies in our power'.

For Auden, Freud's theories were able to explain even the foundations of intellectual enquiry itself, as *New Year Letter* was to indicate by submitting both Marx and Darwin to a Freudian critique. Another German exile in London, Marx in his scholarship brought to consciousness a thought previously unthinkable (not only unacceptable, but quite literally beyond the capacity of thought to envisage). Marx was living out an Oedipal revolt in which the State substituted for the Father, and his frustrated mixed feelings of love and hate burst out in boils as well as economic theory. Darwin suffered pituitary headaches out of guilt at bringing human pride to heel by revealing our kinship with the rest of creation. 'Great sedentary Caesars' who rendered ancient rubbish heaps of thought comprehensible to understanding, all three suffered for their service, becoming that which they opposed. Thus, in Auden's elegy, Freud himself is seen to assume 'the autocratic pose, | the paternal strictness he distrusted'. But each enabled us in different ways to understand and thus control the powers by which we are lived, and their service to human emancipation is unassailable.

The machine economy, *New Year Letter* argues, has replaced the bonds of blood and nation by a personal confederation of subjects whose loyalties are global, not local, and has made us all, in that very Aloneness which is 'man's real condition', potentially members of a single species linked by 'universal,

9

mutual need'. The international transformations of capitalism have made us members of one world, and provided the material means for collective control over it, for the greater good of all. Now only the ideological resistances engendered by short-sighted, sectional self-interest – the false consciousness of nationality, class, and gender – stand in the way of human liberation. Marx's and Freud's insights into the way the discourses of power appropriate each individual subject can free us from the petty tyrannies of what the Freud elegy calls 'the ancient cultures of conceit' and 'their lucrative patterns of frustration', and help to overthrow 'the monolith | of State' in all our heads.

Only a few months after the Freud elegy, *New Year Letter* is already sceptical of such millenarian hopes, making it clear that it has no illusions about the Soviet Union as a socialist utopia. Nevertheless it ends with an euphoric vision of what still might be, though that prospect shrinks in the concluding imagery to an elusive 'Unicorn among the cedars | To whom no magic charm can lead us' (and the poet has already made it clear that he is no political virgin). Auden's later poetry is often seen as that of a disillusioned idealist, cynically seeking refuge in a world-renouncing Christianity that turns its back on the merely local concerns of justice and equity. But this is unfair to the tenor of his very this-worldly Christianity. Though he may in later years have come close to the 'selfish pink old liberal' predicted and feared in 'Letter to Lord Byron', he never completely abandoned the allegiance to social justice of the 1930s. The moral, ecological and libertarian concerns of his poetry from the 1940s onwards still address, in a different language and a transformed historical context, the issues that had made 'action urgent and its nature clear' during that low dishonest decade. The ideologies changed, but the objects of enquiry remained the same, and the 'I' asking the questions retained some continuity and integrity through all its many nows.

THE VARIOUS TYPES OF BOYS

For Auden, as for Wordsworth, the child is father of the man, whether that man is Hitler or Freud, fascist dictator driving away enlightenment or 'autocratic' doctor serving it, for, in the words of 'Letter to Lord Byron', 'no one thinks unless a complex makes him'. Auden's own complexes, as he acknowledged, were rich and varied. According to this poem, all foreigners agree that Englishmen 'as a nation... suffer from an Oedipus fixation'. This is a bit of a joke, which subverts the idea of national uniqueness (and reciprocal national slanders) at the moment that it vaunts them, for of course Freud saw the Oedipus complex as a universal human condition. But every Oedipus complex is different in its particulars and some are very odd indeed. Auden, addressing England as his 'Mater' in these final stanzas of his poem, casts his own artist's variant, with a sly nudge about his sexuality, as 'the queerest thing'.

In a 1934 essay about his schooldays, Auden offered a thumbnail sketch of his own personality at the time:

> As what one sees depends on what one is, I must begin with a description of myself at that time. The son of book-loving, Anglo-Catholic parents of the professional class, the youngest of three brothers, I was – and in most respects still am – mentally precocious, physically backward, short-sighted, a rabbit at all games, very untidy and grubby, a nail-biter, a physical coward, dishonest, sentimental, with no community sense whatever, in fact a typical little highbrow and difficult child.[7]

Such youthful self-denigration is characteristically Audenish in its resonant metonymies. For Auden, nail-biting was not just a minor bad habit but in some way symptomatic of a whole personality. In the poem 'Sir, no man's enemy', for example, he spoke of 'the liar's quinsy', drawing on Layard's belief that a physical illness was a psychosomatic symptom expressing a desire or moral failing, the liar's unconscious punishing him with loss of voice.

Equally characteristic is the self-consciousness about his own status as a socially constructed being. It is not his uniqueness, as one of the century's leading poets, which concerns him, but his typicality, as the representative of an important fraction, the intelligentsia, of a major class, the professional petty bourgeoisie. Auden stands back from his inheritance, which he recognizes not just as a social and cultural environment but as something infolded in the very fabric of his subjectivity.

'Letter to Lord Byron' deposes his own pretensions to

11

specialness by noting that his passport gives his height, colour of hair and eyes and place of birth, but 'With no distinctive markings anywhere'. In Iceland, he says, he recognizes his own stereotypical ancestry in both language and the language of the genes: his name occurs in several of the sagas and is still common throughout the island, while his physical features are commonplace: 'the great big white barbarian, | The Nordic type, the too too truly Aryan'. Elsewhere in the poem, however, his childhood precocity and capacity to shock the 'grown-ups' (on which he prided himself to the last, in poems such as 'Forty Years On' and 'Epistle to a Godson'), reveal just how unstereotypical he was, in part precisely because of the cool taxonomic gaze he brought to bear on his schoolfellows. The first remark of this precocious 7-year-old at his new school, for example, shocked the matron's monumental poise with the comment: ' "I like to see the various types of boys." '

The key to Auden's intellectual identity can be found in the play between a privileged superior view and the recognition of a generic typicality. His writings regularly operate in the generalizing mode, detecting recurrent types and structures amid the diverse phenomena of personal and social life. His criticism is frequently typological, differentiating patterns of behaviour and attitude as they are reflected in kinds of plot and characterization, as, for example, in his discrimination of various Shakespearian archetypes in the extended essay 'The Shakespearian City', or his contrasts of Tristan and Don Juan, Quixote and Sancho Panza, Faust and Prospero, Caliban and Ariel in such essays as 'The Greeks and Us' and 'Balaam and His Ass'.

The capacity to see particular individuals as representative of general modes of behaviour enables him in a work such as 'The Sea and the Mirror' to write a poetic postscript to *The Tempest* in which each of Shakespeare's characters becomes emblematic of different modes of moral response to a shared destiny. In *New Year Letter* figures from literature, myth and history fulfil the same representative role, sometimes in lists and often in contrasted pairs, as, for example, when he speaks of 'LUTHER's faith and MONTAIGNE's doubt', or 'inventive JEFFERSON' and 'realistic HAMILTON'. Even the capitalization of the names adds to this sense of a generic representativeness. The poetry regularly isolates types or emblems of behaviour and identity

– in this poem, for example, complementing the Commuter with the Pioneer. In the sequence 'Bucolics' he identifies different kinds of personality structure with different landscapes, so that, in 'Lakes', lake-folk 'leave aggression to ill-bred romantics' who haunt 'blasted heaths'; while in 'Mountains', 'it is curious how often in steep places | You meet someone short who frowns, | A type you catch beheading daisies with a stick'. Before the sentence is completed he has gone on to an outrageous generalization which reminds us that perfect monsters like Dracula are bred on mountain crags.

One technique Auden uses early and late to reinforce such a taxonomic approach to human life is the generalizing personification familiar from eighteenth-century verse, often applied to moral qualities which are then given a highly concrete set of features. 'August for the people', for example, speaks of 'Scandal praying with her sharp knees up' and 'Courage to his leaking ship appointed', while the Freud elegy, having referred to 'Hate . . . and his dingy clientele', substitutes a simile for the full Augustan capitalization to speak fetchingly of 'problems like relatives gathered | puzzled and jealous about our dying', and goes on in its closing lines to move from personification ('the household of Impulse') to figures from classical myth who fulfil a similar function ('Eros, builder of cities', 'weeping anarchic Aphrodite').

A related mode of generalization is that of generic categories vividly realized through some metonymic gesture or feature: modern man seen as Disney's Mickey Mouse rather than the old swaggering John Bull in 'Letter to Lord Byron' or the shorthand for a whole epoch's misery listed in *New Year Letter*: 'The Asiatic cry of pain, | The shots of executing Spain', the Abyssinian and Danubian despairs, and so on. This capacity to create human taxonomies from the raw data of history and anthropology allows him to speak in confident shorthand in the same poem of 'Empiric Economic Man' as a specific historical construct and in 'City without Walls' of a mass-produced 'Hobbesian Man'; or whimsically to compare Christian worshippers in 'Whitsunday in Kirchstetten' with the 'car-worshippers' whose seasonal exodus from Vienna is also a cult ritual. It is revealed, too, in the sharply etched cameos of such sonnets as 'The Novelist', 'The Composer', 'The Traveller', and in the conversion of

13

individuals into historically representative figures in the portraits of 'Luther', 'Montaigne', 'A. E. Housman', 'Matthew Arnold' or 'Voltaire at Ferney'. All but the last are sonnets, as if this form gave him the opportunity to produce the definitive thumbnail sketch that summed up a whole epoch and history. With similar confident generalization, vast sweeps of human history and prehistory are surveyed in the sonnet sequence and Commentary of 'In Time of War', or in the even more succinct résumés of 'Thanksgiving for a Habitat', 'Horae Canonicae' and 'Memorial for the City' (for all of which the opening stanzas of 'Spain' provide the precedent).

With such a cast of mind, it was relatively easy for Auden in his new American detachment to switch to the parable mode of *For the Time Being* (1944), with its recreation of all the actors in the Nativity story as representative of a range of moral and intellectual positions, or to the allegoric fixations of *The Age of Anxiety* (1947), with its four characters representing Jung's 'Four Faculties' of the ego, Intuition, Feeling, Sensation, Thought. These four had already appeared under their own names as the concretized abstractions of dwarf, nymph, giant and fairy in *For the Time Being*, describing themselves candidly as 'Invisible phantoms', their various embodiments adapted to each individual humour, 'Beautiful facts or true | Generalizations'.

The last formula sums up the way Auden regularly represents the 'various types' that inhabit his work. Even while paying *Homage to Clio* (1960) as 'Muse of the unique | historical fact', Auden converts the diversity of actual histories into this emblematic classical figure. Poignantly realized, perhaps, Clio is no less a generalization than those generations of despots reduced to 'The Short, The Bald, The Pious, The Stammerer', compounded by history, in these terse epithets, to mere instances of the 'various types of boys'.

AN INTELLECTUAL OF THE MIDDLE CLASSES

Auden submitted his own subjectivity to the same disinterested anthropological type-casting. 'Letter to Lord Byron' projects on to some future socialist society that look of the stranger which will see the real oddity of the 'normal' modern self, once its discursive contexts have been dissolved by time:

A child may ask when our strange epoch passes,
During a history lesson, 'Please, sir, what's
An intellectual of the middle classes? . . .'

This is a neat double take, for this future child will merely express an average puzzlement in asking such a question, taking for granted commonplaces of its own world which are, implicitly, equally transient and ideologically constructed. It must be said that Auden takes a certain sneaky pleasure in submitting middle-class assumptions about unique authentic selfhood to the mass-production model of Henry Ford. In his accounts of the major events of his own life he finds a similar typicality, whether tracing the history of his political development in '1929' and 'August for the people' or of his stylistic conversions in 'A Thanksgiving'. This poem casts his changing poetic mentors as reflectors of a journey from prepubescence to foolish fond old man which is intimately entwined with the great representative transitions of contemporary history.

It was at the liberal public school of Gresham's, Holt, in Norfolk, which he attended between 1920 and 1925, that one such typical transit occurred, when, at the age of 15, he assumed the mantle of an intellectual of the middle classes by starting to write poetry. He gave a brief account of this in 'Letter to Lord Byron' and a fuller one in his inaugural lecture as Professor of Poetry at Oxford University in 1956. An older boy on whom he had a crush (Robert Medley, a socialist free thinker later to become a successful artist) asked him, one afternoon in March 1922, whether he had ever written poetry. Though he never had, he knew at once that this was all he wanted to do: 'the suggestion that I write poetry seemed like a revelation from heaven for which nothing in my past could account' (DH 34).

Laid down here is a pattern that was to recur throughout Auden's life: a chance impulse from without, overloaded with libidinal charge, breaks upon the sense to reveal a hitherto unsuspected but now inevitable destiny. This was to be rationalized in the earliest poetry sometimes as 'luck', sometimes in terms of an Anglo-Saxon concept of 'doom', and, later in the Thirties, in classic Marxist terms as a historical determinism which does not preclude but actually requires personal choice and decisive action. After 1940, it was to be seen in increasingly Christian terms as the operation of *grace*, which

15

breaks into the individual life with stringent demands of responsibility and allegiance, as expounded in *For the Time Being*.

A similar external intervention provoked Auden's break with the traditional poetic styles of Hardy and Edward Thomas, his earliest influences, while he was an undergraduate at Christ Church, Oxford, between 1925 and 1928, where he read first Natural Sciences, then PPE, before taking a Third in English. 'Whatever its character,' Auden was to write in America in the summer of 1940, 'the provincial England of 1907, when I was born, was Tennysonian in outlook; whatever its outlook the England of 1925 when I went up to Oxford was *The Waste Land* in character.'[8] The agent of this conversion, again fostered as much by eros as by politics, was a fellow homosexual undergraduate, Tom Driberg (later a left-wing Labour MP and Soviet/British double agent), who introduced him to the poem shortly after their work in the 1926 General Strike in support of the Miners. The effect was immediate. Auden told his Oxford tutor Nevill Coghill: 'I've been reading Eliot. I now see the way I want to write.'[9]

In a 1943 review Auden indicated, tongue in cheek, roughly what Eliot's poem signified to him as a young man:

> had the undergraduate really read his poem, he would have had to say: 'Now I realize I am not the clever young man I thought, but a senile hermaphrodite. Either I must recover or put my head in the gas-stove.' Instead, of course, he said, 'That's wonderful. If only they would read this, Mother would understand why I can't stay home nights, and Father would understand why I can't hold a job.'[10]

If Auden's reactions to contemporary society were cast in the light of an adolescent *Weltschmerz* derived from *The Waste Land* (what he calls here simply changing one's drug to suit a new climate), the major event which prepared him to see that desolation as his birthright was the outbreak of the Great War in 1914. The social upheavals throughout Europe in its wake transformed the security of his parents' comfortable middle-class world for good. The implications of the war for Auden were, he subsequently believed, as significant in personal as in historic terms. When Auden was seven the war took his father away into the Royal Army Medical Corps for four-and-a-half of the son's most formative years, leaving him in the care of a

16

loving but increasingly eccentric mother – an influence to which he later attributed his homosexuality. An unpublished poem Auden wrote at Christmas 1941 for Chester Kallman, the young American who had become his lover, observes that 'mothers have much to do with your queerness and mine'.[11]

The astonishingly swift elevation, at Oxford, of a 20-year-old undergraduate into the decade's outstanding new talent was effected on the basis of a handful of privately circulated, fiercely obscure poems, clearly influenced by Eliot but already with a distinctive timbre of their own. Some of these were published in the occasional journal *Oxford Poetry* which Auden co-edited, and in a limited private edition by his friend and fellow poet Stephen Spender, at Spender's expense, as *Poems* (1928). Such fame was not exactly spontaneous, but relied to a considerable extent on the hype and evangelizing of a coterie of admirers and acolytes. It was assisted at the national level by Eliot himself, who first published the charade 'Paid on Both Sides' in his journal *The Criterion* and, in his position as Poetry Editor for Faber & Faber, ensured the publication of a remarkable selection of first poems in the volume which immediately established Auden's presence on the literary scene, *Poems* (1930).

At Oxford Auden had been widely perceived as the figurehead of a group of young writers, including Louis MacNeice, Cecil Day Lewis and Stephen Spender, sometimes referred to as 'the Auden gang', or more frequently, in the canard coined by the right-wing South African poet Roy Campbell, as 'MacSpaunday'. Protestations that, until the late 1940s, all four of them had not met together in the same room at the same time carried little weight. The names stuck, and Auden was cast ineluctably as the source of a wholly new, 1930s style of Modernism, the 'Audenesque', which many aspiring young poets sought to imitate. Even after the Second World War, poets such as Philip Larkin had to come to terms with the Auden inheritance before they could shape a style of their own. Auden commented in 1968, of the 'MacSpaunday' jibe, in terms which once again insist upon the socially typecast nature of individual identity:

> Four poets of more or less the same age, from more or less the same social background, confronted by the same historical events, will exhibit certain responses in common, but it should have been

17

obvious that what we happened to have in common was the least interesting thing about us.[12]

Oxford itself received short shrift in a 1937 poem of that name for acting as a forcing-house of just such class-based personality stereotypes, where the university's spurious gravitas goes hand in hand with real self-love, and even the college stones appear utterly satisfied with themselves, in 'quadrangles where Wisdom honours herself'. The implication, that such cultural self-love is sterile and onanistic, leading only to 'the knowledge of death... a consuming love', explains the otherwise unexpected advice offered at the end of 'Get there if you can', that 'If we really want to live' we must 'learn to leave ourselves alone'. What animated such indictments as this, as of 'Letter to Lord Byron' 's mockery of Surrey weekends with the well-to-do, was a fiercely provincial contempt for upper-class metropolitan English culture, seen almost from the outside by the anthropological gaze of the stranger, 'The view from Birmingham'.

2

On the Frontier

ANXIOUS AGES, MARGINAL GRIEFS

After going down from Oxford, Auden spent the years between 1930 and 1935 teaching at private schools in Scotland and Herefordshire. It was while he was in his first post at the Larchfield School in Helensburgh, a small ultra-middle-class town on the Clyde, that *Poems* (1930) was published. The hothouse atmosphere of the small private school in an inturned community is curiously fused with the obscure narrative of a politically ambiguous officers' *coup* led by a mysterious Airman in that strange 'postmodernist' *mélange adultère* of prose and verse *The Orators*, which he wrote here in 1931. The book, ironically subtitled *An English Study*, looks in on Englishness from the Scottish sidelines to take as one of its themes the idea that 'The marginal grief | Is source of life'.

Looking in from the margins was to become Auden's most characteristic stance, revealed in his frequent use of the adverb 'between', and accounting for his most famous motif, represented by the title of his last play, written during 1937–8, *On the Frontier*, but also by the opening line of his earliest published poem, written in Zagreb in 1927, 'On the frontier at dawn getting down'. Auden later wrote that *The Orators* was 'meant to be a critique of the fascist outlook but from its reception among my contemporaries and on rereading it myself, I see that it can, most of it, be interpreted as a favorable exposition' (*EA*, p. xv). In the early Thirties, the first frontier he had to cross was in his own head.

The mood of *Poems*, already apparent in the 1928 pamphlet and accentuated by the seven poems added to the 1933 edition, is caught in the unrhymed sonnet to be found in all three volumes, later called 'The Secret Agent'.[1] In this poem the

19

trained spy, alone in enemy territory, warns that trouble is coming; he knows that the key to success lies in control of the passes; he also knows that his urgent wires will be ignored and the bridges remain unbuilt, so that the final sacrifice of his life will have been useless. The effectiveness of the poem lies in the way it seamlessly fuses a vision of a social order in crisis with the delineation of a psychological state of acute anxiety and frustrated action.

In other poems the self's exterior nonchalance conceals the fact that it is forever 'poised between shocking falls on razor-edge', in a 'balancing subterfuge' which maintains the 'accosting profile' and 'erect carriage' ('A Free One') of the ruling class, while all the time frozen into a hysteric composure, 'Hermetically sealed with shame' ('The Questioner Who Sits So Sly'), experiencing 'central anguish felt | For goodness wasted at peripheral fault' ('Venus Will Now Say a Few Words'), and seized by all the psychosomatic symptoms of 'immeasurable neurotic dread', fugues, irregular breathing, mania, the classic fatigue ('Consider').

Recurrently, the self of these early poems is exposed at moments of hesitation and breakdown, by images of stumbling, stammering, stuttering or faltering, as in 'Taller To-day'. Many of the poems speak of the self as an already posthumous creature, a ghost haunted by a loss all the more terrifying for lacking any definition. (See, for example, 'Missing', 'This Loved One', 'Family Ghosts', 'This Lunar Beauty' and 'Paid on Both Sides'.) At times, this can lead the poet to think in terms of a doom like that Anglo-Saxon concept invoked in 'Doom is dark and deeper than any sea-dingle', with its prayer to malign or indifferent powers to protect 'His anxious house ... From gradual ruin spreading like a stain'.

The subsequent title of the last poem, 'The Wanderer', suggests one half of the restless, displaced vagrancy of these poems, the other half of which is summed up in the title later bestowed on a contemporary poem, 'No Change of Place'. At first sight, the two ideas appear contradictory. In fact the nightmare anxiety of these poems is the symptom of a crisis in which the self, driven by some inner urge to escape, transgressing limits, finds an immovable force blocking the way. 'Who will endure', the second poem asks, discovering in its opening anonymous pronoun the inexplicably thwarted and threatened self which is the answer to the rhetorical question. Frozen between the urge to escape and an almost reassuring conviction that all effort is vain, amidst a scene which changes rapidly from summer content to images of autumnal abandonment, this subject is beset by unheeded messages of disaster. None dare venture beyond railhead or pier, while in the foothills a gamekeeper with dog and gun waits to shout 'Turn back!' to anyone foolish enough to attempt escape.

It is not difficult to see this as the figure of a repressive patriarchal power, denying self-realization (including homosexual fulfilment) to the new young self. 'Paid on Both Sides' records the consequences for the sons of a blood feud inherited from generations of forefathers and perpetuated by obsessed mothers. Brooding over these writings is what 'Now from my window-sill' calls 'the long still shadow of the father'. The poem's revised version offers a powerful generalized image of patriarchal invigilation as 'The Watchers', those 'Lords of Limit... | From whom all property begins'. The revision omits the original link with the world of school, which had cast them as the 'Oldest of masters, whom the schoolboy fears', but it retains their dream connection with 'The stocky keepers of a wild estate':

> With guns beneath your arms, in sun and wet,
> At doorways posted or on ridges set,
> By copse or bridge we know you there
> Whose sleepless presences endear
> Our peace to us with a perpetual threat.

These Lords of Limit repress and sustain ('endear' is a significant word). They are, in fact, indispensable to human life. Without them demarcations of property, social order, or precision in action or thought would not be possible. Without the superego, the unconscious id could never be shaped into an articulate, self-directing ego. But in the process of constructing the conscious subject they constrict carnal being within conventional stereotypes of morality and social identity. Using the same gamekeeper image, Caliban, the hyper-articulate spokesman of the id in 'The Sea and the Mirror' (1945), sees them as the very custodians of separate identity, setting those frontiers which delimit the self:

21

For without these prohibitive frontiers we should never know who we were or what we wanted. It is they who donate to neighbourhood all its accuracy and vehemence. It is thanks to them that we do know with whom to associate.... It is thanks to them, too, that we know against whom to rebel. We *can* shock our parents by visiting the dives below the railway track....[2]

At times, the subject of the early poems identifies with the frustrate self who wants to cross the frontier, but is betrayed by his base, as in 'The Secret Agent'. At other times he seems a smugly detached observer haranguing others, like an Old Testament prophet or Eliot's Tiresias:

> Do not imagine you can abdicate;
> Before you reach the frontier you are caught;
> Others have tried it and will try again
> To finish that which they did not begin.

This is from a 1929 poem whose later title, 'Venus Will Now Say a Few Words', explicates its otherwise obscure conviction that the evolutionary process itself, represented by the goddess of fertility, supports the great social changes afoot, which threaten the foundations of capitalist society. 'Consider' starts in the supercilious detachment of the hawk or airman, warning that 'The game is up' and 'It is later than you think'. But, before the end, stasis has been restored to this world in crisis, and the indicter finds himself caught up in the paralysis of which he speaks, even as he warns that 'You cannot be away then... | Not though you pack to leave within the hour'. The poems enact that 'moment of recognition... when the revolutionary change happens and the false concept is abandoned with the realization that it always was false' of which Auden was to write in 'The Greeks and Us' (*FA* 28). The spurious divorce of observer and observed, addresser and addressee, is part of the problem, for the recriminator is himself one of the 'ruined boys' spoken of in 'Consider'. He too cannot abdicate but must try to finish what he did not begin, suffer the loss he fears like those 'Holders of one position, wrong for years', his predecessors.

Before 1929 the self in Auden's poems suffers the deadlock of what 'Family Ghosts' calls 'Massive and taciturn years, the Age of Ice'. By 1932 there is almost gleeful relief at the prospect of ruin, as in 'The Witnesses''s prophecy that 'something is going to fall like rain | and it won't be flowers'. 'August for the people' in Auden's next volume, *Look, Stranger!* (1936), recalls this whole period as one in which 'Our hopes were set still on the spies' career'. Now he envisages a different vocation for the writer, in what is clear to all as an 'hour of crisis and dismay'. That role, exemplified by Isherwood's work, is to 'Make action urgent and its nature clear'. Previous poems had been haunted by the enormity of the task, exhibiting a sense of failure before starting because the anguished subject could not himself see a clear way through or because those to be warned were too absorbed in 'the colours and the consolations, | The showy arid works' to listen. In August 1935, however, the pianos are closed and a clock strikes in earnest of a new and more urgent time. The 'Age of Ice' is over; the glacier has begun to thaw:

> And all sway forward on the dangerous flood
> Of history, that never sleeps or dies,
> And, held one moment, burns the hand.

This is that 'History the operator, the | Organiser, Time the refreshing river' shortly to be invoked in *Spain* (1937). It can be grasped only when the marginal griefs of solitary individuals are transformed from isolated 'moments of tenderness' or 'hours of friendship' into the collective long-term commitment of 'a people's army'. What made the difference for Auden, at this watershed of crisis and dismay, was the discovery of a discourse that could explain a disintegrating world. It required him to cross both literal and metaphoric frontiers.

DEATH OF THE OLD GANG

Social and sexual anxieties coincide in Auden's early poems, in which the gender ambivalence of a Tiresias is as important as the terminal sterility and emptiness of the world he indicts. The apocalyptic imagery, often from Biblical prophecy, extends Eliot's gleeful denunciations into a specifically economic and political critique of his times.

In 1965 Auden recalled, of his youth:

> We were far too insular and preoccupied with ourselves to know or care what was going on across the Channel. Revolution in Russia,

inflation in Germany and Austria, Fascism in Italy, whatever hopes and fears they may have raised in our elders, went unnoticed by us. Before 1930 I never opened a newspaper.[3]

For the young Auden the frontier he had to cross before he could wake from somnambulism to inspect his own culture from the outside was that of a Germany which, in the last days of the Weimar Republic, exhibited a promiscuity of sexual and social lifestyle undreamt of by a provincial middle-class youth.

'Letter to Lord Byron' sees Auden's visit to Berlin in 1929 as a key stage in his odyssey, leading to a conversion described in terms which recall St Augustine in *The Waste Land*:

> Then to Berlin, not Carthage, I was sent
> With money from my parents in my purse,
> And ceased to see the world in terms of verse.

A 1930s readership would see these other terms as political ones; but politics was only part of his 'conversion'. Auden remains silent about what Augustine calls 'a cauldron of unholy loves'. A major element of Berlin's attraction was that decadence recorded by Isherwood in *Mr Norris Changes Trains* (1935), *Sally Bowles* (1937), and *Goodbye to Berlin* (1939), and the play and film *Cabaret* adapted from them. A famous sentence from the last of these novels, 'I am a camera with its shutter open, quite passive, recording, not thinking', was to draw Auden's direct refutation at the start of his 1949 poem about a Berlin divided by the Iron Curtain, 'Memorial for the City'. Nevertheless, it is an accurate description of the 'New Objectivity' (a Weimar catchphrase) Auden brought to bear on Europe in the early 1930s.

Auden still saw the world in terms of verse, but the interpretative model had changed. Prepared to think the worst of western civilization by *The Waste Land*, he now found a mentor to confirm all his deepest suspicions: Bertolt Brecht, the Communist poet and playwright, whose *Threepenny Opera* he saw performed during his Berlin residence. A late poem, 'A Thanksgiving', records this as one in a series of conversions in which he learnt to interpret the world differently through a new literary style. In his prepubescent years he had thought natural landscapes sacred and people rather profane, and Hardy, Edward Thomas and Frost were his mentors. When, an adolescent, he fell in love, Yeats and Robert Graves replaced them. But then (confirming the receptive passivity of his idea of conversion),

> without warning, the whole
> Economy suddenly crumbled:
> there to instruct me was Brecht.

On 'Black Friday', 28 October 1929, the Wall Street Crash inaugurated the chronic economic collapse of the Depression years. The consequent mass unemployment fostered the advance of Fascism and Communism throughout Europe and confirmed the darkest predictions about the destiny of capitalism. The four-part poem later called '1929' charts his growing awareness of the historical roots of identity, and the stages of conversion recalled in 'A Thanksgiving'. At the start clouds move untroubled across an open sky – unlike the 'frightened soul' who, seeing even fallen bicycles as 'huddled corpses', suffers 'anxiety at night, | Shooting and barricade in street', shares a friend's hysteria, and feels the 'restlessness of intercepted growth'. The way forward is foreshadowed by 'the loud madman' sinking into 'a more terrible calm', as the sequence moves from political naïvety, distressed on his Eastertime arrival in Germany at the plight of the unemployed, street demonstrations and police brutality, to pronounce in October with the glee of the convert that 'It is time for the destruction of error'.

This revolutionary break with the past can be accomplished only in a death and rebirth like that of which St Paul speaks in 1 Corinthians. (The passage was read at Auden's funeral in 1973.[4]) It requires not only 'Death of the old gang' but 'death of the grain, our death', since bourgeois individuals like himself carry the corruption within them. (In Berlin in 1929, Auden had been visited by a badly wounded John Layard, who begged him to finish off a bungled suicide attempt. Wisely, Auden called an ambulance.[5])

The subject of the early writings repeatedly realizes his own complicity with that which he rejects, fearing that even in rejection he perpetuates it. In The Orators, the 'Enemy' establishment triumphs by infecting the rebel Airman with its own death wish. The Old Boy who delivers an 'Address for a Prize Day' asks, rhetorically, 'What do you think about England, this country of ours where nobody is well?' By 1930, Auden thought he had the answer, drawing on the theories of psychosomatic illness propounded by Layard and Gerald Heard, derived from Georg Groddeck's and Homer Lane's eccentric adaptations of Freud.

In 'Psychology and Art To-day' Auden argued that 'all illness is purposive. It is an attempt at cure. All change, either progressive or regressive is caused by frustration or tension.'[6] What the early poems saw as part of the problem, the condition of a young proud stranger 'frustrate and vexed' before a resistant world, has now been redefined as part of the solution, for frustrated energy accumulates until it breaks through into qualitative change. The illness is symptom but also sign of what has to be cured, like Marx's boils and Darwin's headaches, Miss Gee's ovarian cancer, the child of her repressed procreative impulse, or the Airman's kleptomania and onanism, symptoms of a self-consuming capitalism where conspicuous consumption and self-abuse are related sicknesses.

Otherwise, as in 'Get there if you can', one is simply waiting for the end, hearing 'doom's approaching footsteps' as the mob prepares to blow up the whole show. This poem had stressed the speaker's complicity in the collapse he proclaims, surreptitiously converting 'you' into 'we'; but the real source of corruption is a profiteering 'they', a *rentier* class living off rents and interest and the earnings of others:

Far from there we spent the money, thinking we could well afford,
While they quietly undersold us with their cheaper trade abroad.

Death of the Old Gang requires 'our death' also, for the 'Enemy' of *The Orators*, the 'supreme Antagonist' of 'Consider', has set up house right in the heart of the bourgeois individual, and only the willed spiritual suicide of the 'ruined boys', to be reborn in a new, collective identity, can save the show. 'Paid on Both Sides' had depicted a generation in futile revolt against the patriarchal inheritance which condemned them to blood feud and vendetta. By the time of the plays he co-authored with Christopher Isherwood, *The Dog Beneath the Skin* (1935), *The Ascent of F6* (1936) and *On the Frontier* (1938), this antagonism is self-consciously played out in the terms of an Oedipal revolt against the fathers. Each of these plays is a parable of conversion

26

in which freedom is found only in rejection of one's patrimony, symbolically killing the father by opting for 'the other side', crossing the frontier.

For all Auden's later protestations to the contrary, it is difficult not to see these plays as influenced by Brecht's idea of the 'alienation effect', so consonant with Auden's tendency to stand back from experience and note its socially constructed, 'artificial' nature. 'Paid on Both Sides' had already achieved this effect by overlaying the language and mores of Icelandic saga, public-school camaraderie and gangster fiction in one anachronistic scenario. But by the time of *The Dance of Death* (1933) it is clear that the German experience has given him a language of estrangement with which to register his sense of the oddity and artifice of bourgeois life.

The secret that must out in this play is pronounced by the BBC Announcer at the start: 'We present to you this evening a picture of the decline of a class, of how its members dream of a new life, but secretly desire the old, for there is death inside them. We show you that death as a dancer.' Throughout the play, Death dances on, through Charleston rhythms, audience interventions and walkouts, cabaret turns and burlesque versions of history. The play alludes not only to medieval reactions to the plague but to a contemporary symptom of the Depression years, those dance marathons in which couples competed for money prizes up to and beyond the point of physical exhaustion. The dancer is forced constantly to update his increasingly frenetic routines to meet changing circumstances, and to keep his audience hypnotized with admiration, till he collapses. In the same way, capitalism's multitudes have 'ruined each other for they didn't know how | They were making the conditions that are killing them now'. If Auden and his fellow intellectuals belong to the doomed rentier class indicted here, they also yearn ardently to renounce it. Brecht's formal innovations carried with them a political baggage. After October 1929, only Communism seemed to offer a passport across the frontier.

THE GIFT OF DOUBLE FOCUS

While a teacher at the Downs School, Auden wrote in the

summer of 1933 another poem which moves from a little arena of comfort and security amidst a mutually supportive, privileged group of friends and fellow teachers to a cold, distressing vision of the exploitation on which that privilege is founded. 'Out on the lawn' begins amidst 'the sexy airs of summer' in 'gardens where we feel secure'; but its viewpoint shifts to the cold, estranging gaze of the moon, staring 'blankly as an orphan' on the churches, power stations and art galleries of a self-satisfied civilization. By the end, hungry multitudes have gathered outside the walls where 'we | Whom hunger cannot move' endure the self-indulgent pangs of personal love,

> And, gentle, do not care to know,
> Where Poland draws her Eastern bow,
> What violence is done;
> Nor ask what doubtful act allows
> Our freedom in this English house,
> Our picnics in the sun.

There is in this poem what Auden was to call, in *New Year Letter*, 'the gift of double focus'. For if, on the one hand, he takes pleasure in 'these evenings when | Fear gave his watch no look', he also looks askance at this comfortable world, feeling that its privilege deserves to be engulfed by the 'crumpling flood' of revolution. Even the word 'gentle' partakes of this double focus. The genuine gentleness of their 'kindness to ten persons' is possible only because of their exclusive, well-heeled gentility. Beneath the bland bourgeois surfaces, as *The Ascent of F6* proclaimed, 'There is always another story, there is more than meets the eye', a 'wicked secret' which 'September 1, 1939' identifies as 'Imperialism's face, | And the international wrong'. The oppressor's face is there revealed as the poet's own, staring back from the bar mirror as he and his companions try to drink themselves into a forgetful 'euphoric dream', the beneficiaries of a system for which, now, the price has to be paid.

'A mind which entertains a false concept', Auden was to write in 'The Greeks and Us',

> may be brought through steps of argument to entertain the true one, but this does not mean that a false concept has grown into the true; there is always a point in the dialectic, like the moment of recognition in tragedy, when the revolutionary change happens

and the false concept is abandoned with the realization that it always was false. The dialectic process may take time, but the truth it discovers has no history.[7]

Such double focus requires 'a tremendous feat of moral courage and discipline', overcoming natural anxiety to look at one's self and one's world with the eye of a stranger. Without this self-estrangement 'we would never have become fully conscious, which is to say that we would never have become, for better or worse, fully human'.[8] This is covert autobiography, speaking of those crises of consciousness Auden was to record in 'Thanksgiving', two in particular: his conversion to a form of Communism and his return to the Anglican Christianity of his childhood.

The middle class, Auden wrote in a 1929 journal, is an 'orphan class, with no fixed residence, capable of snobbery in both directions' (EA 299). For the young Auden, the family was an apparatus for creating pliant subjects, and 'perfect pater' and 'marvellous mother', the domestic agents of 'Them'. His essay in Graham Greene's collection The Old School argued that the public-school system is an ideological forcing-house, not only in the conscious propagation of beliefs but in its power to police the inner consciousness and even the unconscious of its pupils. His schooldays, he says, orchestrated a 'moral life ... based on fear, on fear of the community', and this is 'not a healthy basis. It makes one furtive and dishonest and unadventurous.' Hyperbolically, he claims that 'at school I lived in a Fascist state' (EA 325). The unequal relations of power are 'What all school-children learn', according to 'September 1, 1939'. Schools not only impart information, they also communicate attitudes, feelings and ways of seeing deformed by class interest, so that

> it is impossible to see how any school ... where boys and staff are both drawn from the monied classes, can hope to see the world picture of that class objectively. The mass production of gentlemen is their *raison d'être*, and one can hardly suggest that they should adopt principles which would destroy them. (EA 322-3)

Elsewhere he argues that the Renaissance ideal of the gentleman scholar 'encouraged speculation at the expense of authority, but it only intensified the gulf between thought and action, by making learning an aristocratic privilege', creating an illusion of 'disinterested knowledge', divorced from action and social responsibility, which comes close to being the ideological cloak of 'the *rentier* who is free to devote himself to higher things'.[9] Yet a similar disinterestedness provokes the youthful defections to the workers' cause in *The Dog Beneath the Skin*, the revolt against their families' rival nationalisms of the young lovers in *On the Frontier*, and even the anti-political mysticism and suicide of Ransom in *The Ascent of F6*. The dilemma of Auden's whole left-leaning generation is summed up by the title he later gave to an Ode in *The Orators* addressed 'To My Pupils': 'Which side am I supposed to be on?' The 'double focus' here reveals much more than the predicament of a progressive teacher in a conservative school system. A rather more perplexing question than 'Which side am I on?', it explains much of that dilatory hovering on the frontier, that readiness to listen to the injunction ' "Turn back!" ', of the Thirties poetry.

PRIVATE STUFF AND PUBLIC SPIRIT

'No Change of Place' merges spiritual and economic conversions, lamenting that 'No one will ever know | For what conversion brilliant capital is waiting'. The poem echoes Augustine ('Place is there none; we go backward and forward, and there is no place'), Marlowe's Mephistopheles ('For where we are is Hell, nor are we out of it'), and Milton's Satan ('nor from Hell | One step no more than from Himself can fly | By change of place'). What the rebellious son experiences here is that mixture of Luciferian dread and desire involved in the transgression of patriarchal limits. An early review adapts St Paul to explain the psychology of modern revolt. Political, like spiritual conversion issues from a 'duality... between the whole self at different stages of development – e.g. a man before and after a religious conversion. The old life must die in giving birth to the new. That which desires life to itself... casts itself, like Lucifer, out of heaven.'[10] Auden wrote in a 1929 journal that 'the real "life-wish" is the desire for separation, from family, from one's literary predecessors' (*EA* 299). By the time of *Look, Stranger!* that Luciferian 'life-wish' required an even more radical estrangement, from its own culturally constructed subjectivity, expressed everywhere in a Pauline rhetoric of conversion which affirms continuity as it speaks of schism.

The volume's 'Prologue' invokes a new order of solidarity addressed in a Communist remake of Pauline 'Charity' as 'O Love, the interest itself in thoughtless Heaven'. The volume overflows with embarrassing vocatives and visions of 'universal love'. Such spilt Christian visions are not, however, without a certain Leninist rigour. 'Prologue''s 'possible dream' of a different kind of future requires that on 'our talk and kindness' Communism lays 'Its military silence, its surgeon's idea of pain', hurting to heal. The full version of 'Out on the Lawn' has the same ambivalence. The moon is an orphan, but so too, in prospect, is the poet. After the deluge, a convoluted simile suggests, 'The drowned voices of his parents' may rise again 'In unlamenting song' through 'a child's rash happy cries'. But not even subliminal Oedipal glee can dispel the fear that rashness will bring only desolation masquerading as peace. The new world to emerge once the revolution's 'crumpling flood' destroys 'the dykes of our content' with visions of 'sudden death' may be a utopia. The privacy they dread to lose may be compensated for by the 'strength' to which they now 'belong'. But that last word sets off all sorts of anxieties revealed subliminally in images of stranded, gasping sea monsters, murderer and pouncing tigress. If this poem affirms, as Auden later suggested (FA 69–70), a vision of *Agape*, it is one shot through with the dubious erotics of the death wish.

Auden in 1932 confided to a current lover, the poet John Pudney, that 'groups and sex... complement each other like day and night.... We're all sex-obsessed today because there isn't any decent group life left hardly'.[11] *The Orators* had nominated as 'the crucial problem – group organisation'. In 1934 he contributed an essay on 'The Group Movement and the Middle Classes' to a collection edited by another occasional lover, Richard Crossman, arguing that the 'psychological importance of the small group' lay in allowing the individual 'to lose himself, for his death instincts to be neutralized' and used creatively for the good of the collectivity.[12] In *Look, Stranger!*, 'Brothers, who when the sirens roar' already partially retreats from the declarative Communism of its original publication, which began with a rousing 'Comrades', under the combative

31

title 'A Communist to Others'.[13] The poem proposes a fraternal comradeship of workers and intellectuals infused by the homoerotic pantheism of Walt Whitman; but it omits the original frank appeal to those 'Brothers for whom our bowels yearn', joined by a 'Love outside our own election'.

Summing up this fashionable collectivism, Louis MacNeice's contribution to *The Arts To-day* observed that the 'personal obsession' of Auden, Spender and Day Lewis 'can be collated with their joint communist outlook via the concept of comradeship.... Comradeship is the communist substitute for bourgeois romance; in its extreme form (cp. also fascism and youth-cults in general) it leads to an idealisation of homosexuality.'[14] By contrast, Auden's poem later called 'A Bride in the 30s' recognizes that the desire to love and be loved may be abused for sinister ends, speaking of the 'wooing poses' of dictator and demagogue, seducing the populace with fantasies of fulfilment and belonging. Another poem, 'Now the leaves are falling fast', contrasts the loveless solitude of hands freezing 'Lonely on the separate knees' with the spurious solidarities of mass society, 'Arms raised stiffly' in unison in what could be Nazi or Communist salutes, but which are certainly 'false attitudes of love'.

As Auden was to acknowledge, in part by suppressing, doctoring and apologizing for some of these conspicuously 'political' poems, dictators of the left such as Stalin were as unscrupulous as 'Hitler and Mussolini in their wooing poses' in manipulating the urge to belong of déraciné Western intellectuals. Some of the finest poems in the volume arise from the conflict between the public values Auden wants to espouse and the personal fears and anxieties that actually grip him. It is not that he is really a poet of private passion momentarily hijacked into public attitudes by an importunate history. Rather his greatness lies in capturing for all time the divided loyalties and torn emotions of an era when, in the words of Thomas Mann, quoted by Yeats as epigraph to one of his last poems, 'In our time the destiny of man presents its meaning in political terms'. For Auden this was embodied practically in his 1935 marriage to Mann's daughter Erika, a lesbian, to facilitate her departure from Nazi Germany.

The best poems in *Look, Stranger!* stress the inseparability of private and public spheres, complicating the idea of a love that 'through our private stuff must work | His public spirit' with an insight into what 'A Bride in the 30s' calls 'The power that corrupts, that power to excess | The beautiful quite naturally possess', in a world 'Where the engaging face is the face of the betrayer'. Love, the poem says, merging collective and individual drives, is without 'opinions' or a 'programme' of its own (both words suggesting an insistent public world); it 'Will do no trick' (a highly dismissive formula) 'except at our proposal'. The poem ends with a warning that looks forward to the key proposition of Auden's most overtly 'political' poem, that the life choice remains with each individual, whether phrased in the language of learning or the language of love. In 'Fleeing the short-haired mad executives', the escapism of personal love ends in disillusion, recognizing that 'Love gave the power, but took the will'. A similar disenchantment pervades such sonnets as 'A shilling life' and 'Love had him fast', with its suffocation and constriction and 'hopeful falsehood', as it does the misery and betrayal in a cavernous railway terminus crowded with displaced persons of the haunting dream poem, 'Dear, though the night is gone'. The public desolation of this *mise-en-scène* indicates the real arena of distress as much as hope in these poems, confirmed in the 'Epilogue', where not love but hatred has the final word on a planet inhabited by the dead, where 'the wish to wound has the power'.

For all its over-insistent celebration of those, including Freud, Groddeck and D. H. Lawrence, who, unlearning hatred, have turned their faces towards a better world (one discreetly identified as Communist by oblique allusion to an unnamed Lenin), this last poem sees the planet hurling headlong towards disaster. There is now no separation of privileged observer from the observed masses: we ourselves are part of that crowd wooed and terrified by rumour as in any Shakespeare play. 'The betrayers thunder at, blackmail | Us', the delay of the enjambement giving us pause at our own complicity. Now every comforter is really a liar, for if we are, in bourgeois self-congratulation, 'the conscious-stricken', we are also 'the weapon-making', and all our affluent modernity is sustained by the city's 'byres of poverty'. This is a world where 'The feverish prejudiced lives do not care...lost' in 'the glittering | Brass of the great retreat' (the isolation of 'lost' at the line-ending taking on a full Christian resonance).

The brass bands, like the 'flutter of bunting' of which the poem also speaks, make clear what this 'great retreat' is. Auden had described it in a 1934 review in *Now and Then* (*EA* 320–1) as 'an escape from reason and consciousness... to enlist in the great Fascist retreat which will land us finally in the ditch of despair'. The review finds both the 'Western-romantic conception of personal love' and the Laurentian cult of sexual liberation wanting, 'a neurotic symptom only inflaming our loneliness, a bad answer to our real wish to be united and rooted in life'. They simply 'postpone a cure'. The 'way back to real intimacy', it proposes, lies through a 'kind of asceticism': 'The self must first learn to be indifferent; as Lenin said, "To go hungry, work illegally and be anonymous."' The sexually and politically ambivalent T. E. Lawrence ('Lawrence of Arabia'), it argues, is another figure of such ascetism, his life 'an allegory of the transformation of the Truly Weak Man into the Truly Strong Man, an answer to the question "How shall the self-conscious man be saved?"' He and Lenin are 'the two whose lives exemplify most completely what is best and significant in our time, our nearest approach to a synthesis of feeling and reason, act and thought, the most potent agents of freedom and to us, egotistical underlings, the most relevant accusation and hope'. One of the most famous lyrics in *Look, Stranger!*, 'Our hunting fathers', picks up the phrase attributed to Lenin in this review, to reject a liberal tradition founded on personal glory, appetite and power, and the godlike conviction of rightness, in the name of a different love, 'one suited to | The intricate ways of guilt'. Transgressing the name of the Father, the Communist convert can become the Truly Strong Man only by learning 'To think no thought but ours, | To hunger, work illegally, | And be anonymous.'

Everywhere in *Look, Stranger!* this conversion is identified with the reinvention of a self which will find liberation only in the 'synthesis of feeling and reason, action and thought' offered by a political engagement; for, in the closing words of the subsequently suppressed 'Here on the cropped grass', paraphrasing *The Communist Manifesto*, real community is found only in collective action:

> These moods give no permission to be idle,
> For men are changed by what they do;
> And through loss and anger the hands of the unlucky
> Love one another.

That phrase about 'think[ing] no thought but ours' indicates where the flaw lies for an Auden who, in theory at least, passionately wants to be changed by what he does. 'The danger of [D. H.] Lawrence's writing is the ease with which his teaching about the unconscious, by which he means the impersonal unconscious, may be read as meaning, "let your personal unconscious have its fling"', he wrote in 'Psychology and Art To-day'. While in personal relations this 'may have a liberating effect for the individual', it is 'rotten political advice, where it means "beat up those who disagree with you"', leading to fascist cults of violence as liberation.[15] Auden never joined the Communist Party, though the politics of *Look, Stranger!* and subsequent 1930s volumes closely shadow its 'Popular Front' programme, nowhere more than in the fudging sentimentality which elides 'universal love' with rather more stringent ideas of political solidarity and action.

As early as 1932 Michael Roberts had written of the Auden generation's combination of 'a revolutionary attitude with a respect of eighteenth-century ideals', evincing an 'impersonality [which] comes not from extreme detachment but from solidarity with others', something 'nearer to the Greek conception of good citizenship than to the stoical austerity of recent verse'.[16] But for all this poetry's ambition to be (in Roberts's words) 'popular' and 'contemporary', a Stalinized Communist movement demanded much more: the submission of individual conscience and intellectual honesty to every opportunist twist and turn of a *soi-disant* 'impersonal' and 'objective' Party orthodoxy. Even toughly political writers such as Auden's friend Edward Upward (dedicatee of an ode in *The Orators*) found this increasingly difficult to accept, and well-nigh impossible by the time of the Nazi–Soviet Pact. In Spain in 1937 Auden was to find his own personal sticking-point.

3

Truth is Elsewhere

The traveller's hope at the start of *Letters from Iceland* (1937) was to be 'far from any | Physician', free from the need for a healer. The internationalism of 'Journey to Iceland' rejects all local allegiances, convinced that history has also rejected them: 'our time has no favourite suburb', and the 'fabulous | Country' of some utopian future is 'impartially far' from all parochial addresses. In the words of *On the Frontier*: 'Truth is elsewhere.' Reality is characterized, that is, by a determinate absence: that which is most central to it is missing, an unrealized negativity. The same year that *Letters from Iceland* was published, however, history nominated one favourite place and time, and Auden followed it there: Spain, 1937. In 'Journey to Iceland', 'North means to all: "Reject!"'; but the command of *Spain* (1937) is to *join*.

The poem emphasizes the freedom of the individual to choose a destiny in terms which prefigure the Kierkegaardian turn of *New Year Letter*. The life force says to each 'I am your choice, your decision', challenging them to bring the potential into existence. But that freedom is soon imprisoned in necessity, demanding from each allegedly free subject the 'conscious acceptance of guilt in the necessary murder' which seems the inevitable consequence of political commitment. This is the modern dilemma expressed as paradox in *Journey to a War* (1939): 'We live in freedom of necessity.'

Auden here sees his trip to China with Isherwood as a stage on the road to that global conflict which finally erupted in September 1939. *New Year Letter*, completed by October 1940 in a still neutral USA, assumes rather more necessity and less freedom for the self, observing that 'we are conscripts to our age' and 'No words men write can stop the war', but finding also the 'immeasurable grief' of its outbreak a relief from the anxiety of expectation. The poem ends with a wishful vision of a republic 'Where Freedom dwells because it must, | Necessity because it can, | And men confederate in Man'. But in retrospect what seems most nearly prophetic in this close is its vision of 'A weary Asia out of sight' tugging night's blanket off a restless sleeping America to wake it to a world where 'Ashamed civilians come to grief | In brotherhoods without belief'.

Just over a year later, the Imperial Japanese Airforce bombed the US fleet at Pearl Harbor, and the United States entered the war. *For the Time Being*, first published in 1944 along with 'The Sea and the Mirror', dates from this period, when 'The evil and armed draw near' and 'Alone, alone, about a dreadful wood | Of conscious evil runs a lost mankind'. By the time *The Age of Anxiety* (first published in the United States in 1947) was being composed in the last two years of the war, illusions of personal autonomy and freedom had long vanished into a holocaust where 'Many have perished; more will', the living have been reduced to 'the anxious status of a shady character or a displaced person' and 'even the most prudent become worshippers of chance'. As the book's 'Prologue' makes clear, 'When the historical process breaks down and armies organize ... necessity is associated with horror and freedom with boredom'. The long poems of the 1940s explore the moral and spiritual consequences of a conscription to history that for Auden really began with Spain.

The Spanish Civil War broke out in July 1936 while Auden and MacNeice were still in Iceland. Under the leadership of General Franco and other extreme right-wing 'Nationalist' officers, the Spanish Army rebelled against an elected Republican government which had begun to introduce modest social reforms. The cause of the Spanish Falangists was quickly espoused by Mussolini and Hitler, who despatched several battalions of 'volunteers' in support. The Western democracies, Conservative Britain and Socialist France alike, responded with a Non-Intervention policy which played into the hands of the dictators by embargoing the export of military supplies to either side, when it was the Republic, with its army in revolt, which needed them. Only the Soviet Union offered military support, thereby ensuring that the government coalition fell into Communist hands. At the time, such support seemed like socialist solidarity rather than Stalinist *Realpolitik*. For socialists, liberals and many conservatives in the democracies, as well as for refugees from the fascist countries, Spain became the place where, in the words of *Spain*, 'the menacing shapes of our fever | Are precise and alive', the anxieties of a decade translated into 'invading battalions', and the Old Gang could be seen 'projecting their greed as the firing squad and the bomb'.

Auden spent only a couple of months in Spain, leaving in early March 1937. He had intended to enlist in the International Brigade as an ambulance driver, no doubt influenced by Hemingway's anti-war novel *A Farewell to Arms* (1929). Instead he ended up kicking his heels, as a celebrity whose death the authorities could not afford, in occasional propaganda broadcasting. His poem was published as a fund-raising pamphlet for Medical Aid for Spain in the same month that the Republican government put down the uprising in Barcelona of Anarchist and POUM (left-wing socialist) militias who wanted a more radical programme and an end to Communist domination. George Orwell witnessed the insurrection and wrote about it sympathetically in *Homage to Catalonia* (1938). In *Inside the Whale* (1940) he delivered a vitriolic attack on Auden's poem as a shameless apologia for Stalinism: 'a sort of thumb-nail sketch of a day in the life of a "good party man". In the morning a couple of political murders, a ten-minutes' interlude to stifle "bourgeois" remorse, and then a hurried luncheon and a busy afternoon chalking walls and distributing leaflets.'[1]

Orwell's experience of Comintern-inspired murders within the Republic's own ranks focused his anger on the poem's reference to 'the necessary murder', which, he said, 'could only be written by a person to whom murder is at most a *word*'. Auden subsequently admitted that his own experiences in Spain had left him disillusioned, but that the need to defeat fascism silenced his reservations in the name of a greater good. This does not quite square with the facts: both *Journey to a War* and *Another Time* (1940) still espouse 'left' positions, and the former shows considerable sympathy for the Chinese Communists (disavowed in the 1973 edition), currently fighting a guerrilla war against Japanese invasion. The long meditative 'Commentary' which concludes this volume dissociates itself, certainly, from 'the violent | Who long to calm our guilt with murder'. But the tyrannies which promise 'Unity' at the expense of 'Freedom' and urge 'Leave Truth to the police and us' seem to lie unequivocally on the political right.

By the time Auden republished his poem as 'Spain 1937' in *Another Time* he had revised its offending line to speak only of 'the fact of murder'. After 1950 he dropped it entirely from the canon, describing it in the Foreword to his 1966 *Collected Shorter Poems* as 'dishonest', 'shamefully' expressing a 'wicked doctrine' and 'feelings or beliefs which its author never felt or entertained... simply because it sounded to me rhetorically effective'. The title poem of *Homage to Clio* (1960) may well pay respects to Orwell's Spanish book. Certainly it recalls one of the most graphic images of the Civil War in its depiction of the Muse of History as 'any | Girl no one has noticed', photographed in the newspapers 'nursing | A baby or mourning a corpse'; and it goes on to denounce a world of Stalinist *Realpolitik* where 'Only the first step would count and that | Would always be murder'.

What remains from *Spain* is, however, something different: a sense of the waste and futility of an age in which the dream of universal brotherhood was co-opted by dictatorships of left and right and individuals were left alone with their day, with only the 'makeshift consolations' of a shared cigarette, the masculine jokes and the 'Fumbled and unsatisfactory embrace before hurting'. The poem agonizes over the corruption of such brief moments of solidarity by a brutal politics, desperately trying to hold on to an inheritance which might be lost forever if fascism triumphed. History, says its final line, 'May say Alas but cannot help or pardon' those who fail to act now, in this moment of choice and decision.

NOTHING IS GIVEN

Pardon, as a judicial as well as spiritual concept, recurs frequently in the following years. In *Journey to a War* a Japanese bombing-raid prompts the reflection:

> We live here. We lie in the Present's unopened
> Sorrow; its limits are what we are.
> The prisoner ought never to pardon his cell.

39

Non-combatant tourists, Auden and Isherwood had thought themselves immune, neutral, unengaged. But bombs do not discriminate. Non-involvement is a lie: they have just heard that Hitler has invaded Austria. To accept injustice as a fact of life is to connive in the perpetuation of our prison. Rulers once forged a sense of national identity through 'the Fairly-Noble unifying Lie'. Now such ideologies have degenerated into 'wounded myths that once made nations good', the causes of international disorder in a world where 'the will of the Unjust' holds sway. There is almost a satisfaction in knowing that 'we are going to suffer, now'. The bombers fly over like some return of the repressed, 'ugly long-forgotten memories' which the anti-aircraft guns resist like a newly awakened conscience.

The poem 'They', from *Another Time*, makes the same point. The 'Terrible Presences' that cast the shadow of their crooked wings across our dearest locations have been summoned by our own concupiscence. The beautiful bridegroom of the future yearned for in '1929' has turned up ten years late, but a 'hairy and clumsy bridegroom' from whom our virginal whiteness shrinks in terror, only to 'conceive in the shuddering instant'. The bed has been made, the future conceived by choices we cannot now rescind. Such violence, *Journey to a War* indicates, projects onto a global scale the 'private massacres' and fantasies of vengeance that lurk 'Behind each sociable home-loving eye'. The sequence insists that there is no metaphysical court of appeal: 'The mountains cannot judge us when we lie.' We must judge ourselves. The Japanese 'chose a fate' to which they were not compelled by simple geography. We too may 'turn away from freedom' by failing to resist 'Violence successful like a new disease' with countervailing violence. Ironically, in the 'Commentary' it is the Japanese invader who is 'deadly and impartial as a judge', because his bombs murder rich and poor alike.

The argument of these sonnets, in which Auden contests his own growing attraction to pacificism, still hinges on the idea of the 'necessary murder'. The ideological discourses by which we construct an identity are also those which kill us. But some ideas remain true even though men die for them. There really are 'places | Where life is evil now: | Nanking; Dachau'. We have a duty not to avert our gaze in this year 'When Austria died and China was forsaken, | Shanghai in flames and Teruel re-taken', pretending it has nothing to do with us. Though we can do little individually, we can, like the nameless, dead Chinese peasant-soldier of another sonnet, add 'meaning like a comma' to a collective history.

Paraphrase cannot do justice to the vivid particularity and riddling concision with which the sequence explores the historic intertwining of violence and knowledge, through a series of vignettes, tableaux and character-sketches, from the mythic expulsion from Eden to a present where once more 'Disaster comes' and, 'articled to error', we realize anew our responsibility for it. In this millenial scenario, enlightenment repeatedly disentangles itself from ignorance and superstition, as, in ancient Babylon, astronomy emerged from astrology, and later chemistry from alchemy, physics from metaphysics and medicine from faith-healing, only to be driven away again. History is no uninterrupted progress. Every great intellectual revolution generates the reaction or perversion which will overthrow it. 'The Good Place has not been'; we are 'A race of promise that has never proved its worth'. But for the changeable 'childish creature' of the opening sonnet, looking for truth and continually mistaken, 'On whom the years could model any feature', this very incompleteness is the ground of freedom. As a later sonnet insists, neither the species nor the individual has a preordained destiny: 'Nothing is given: we must find our law.'

The extended 'Commentary' has been widely criticized for its naïve portentousness, but its vision of 'The only animal aware of lack of finish', living in a zone of continual war 'Between the dead and the unborn, the Real and the Pretended', is moving and cogent. '*Jen*, the Truly Human', of the Chinese ideogram may still be 'unachieved'. But its unsuccess is charted in a brilliant résumé of evolution from 'boneless worm-like ancestors', through the growth of the forebrain ('a great success') and the emergence of the species during the Laufen Ice Retreat, to the historical epochs summarized as the Three Great Disappointments: the fall of the Roman Empire, the era of the Universal Churches, and the epoch of Galilean/Cartesian science and humanism which brought it to an end, now playing out its last days. To define these epochs in terms not of their achievements but of what the Yeats elegy calls 'human unsuccess', seeing them as 'United by a common sense of human failure', is a masterstroke of deconstructive irony. It prepares us to confront the Present's unopened present, not with grandiose claims that this time it will be different, but with a resolve stiffened by the fear of yet another failure, in a universe where we are 'both judge and victim'.

The Chinese front is the 'local variant' of a war in which all are implicated, in a world without 'localised events'. It is fought across a university campus and in the laboratory or lovers' bedroom as much as in the defence of Madrid. In this war knowledge is a weapon, and the motif of knowing, learning and teaching is central to the whole sequence. Through intellectual enquiry the great liberators 'took Necessity, and knew her, and she brought forth Freedom', penetrating the lines of ideology, and reconciling in a single equation unity and liberty, justice and truth. There is much that is powerful and moving in this poem, particularly in its precocious ecological emphases, speaking of a planet desecrated by human immoderation, but offering too the prospect of outgrowing our madness. For there is, it insists, still the choice to 'Clear from the head the masses of impressive rubbish', to 'construct at last a human justice' amidst those great trackways of the galaxy where nothing is given, where our 'tribe and truth are nothing'.

KILLING TIME

A 1936 poem, 'Detective Story', had begun in the pastoral tranquillity of an English village only to turn it, by the end of the first paragraph, into the site of a crime, exploiting the traditional association of such scenes with this sub-literary genre to home in on 'the spot | Where the body of [our] happiness was first discovered'. The analogy turns the plotted inevitability of the genre into a parable of personal life, to conclude on a fatalistic double bind:

> But time is always killed. Someone must pay for
> Our loss of happiness, our happiness itself.

The conviction that we shall all have to pay for idly killing time in a time of global killing permeates *Another Time*. The fear of 'September 1, 1939' that Enlightenment will once again be driven away figures equally in 'Voltaire at Ferney', where the ageing philosopher confronts the return of a new dark ages, throughout Europe 'the horrible nurses... | Itching to boil their children'. Near the end of the book the Yeats elegy asserts that 'poetry makes nothing happen'. Here, near its start, Voltaire is convinced that 'Only his verses | Perhaps could stop them'. The carefully placed qualification on the emjambement advises not diffidence but a desperate immodesty: 'He must go on working.' Unlike the doubt-ridden Christian Pascal of the preceding poem, terrified by the eternal silence between the stars, the sceptic Voltaire assumes a universe subject to rational scrutiny where, 'Overhead, | The uncomplaining stars composed their lucid song.' But if 'Civilise' is Voltaire's great injunction, it carries with it no easy confidence, nor does it rule out using all the tricks of 'the false and the unfair' to outwit oppression, whether the 'two-faced answer or the plain protective lie'. The cunning of reason, as in the China sequence, is 'patient like a peasant'.

Patience is set for the long haul, but Voltaire here is already near the end, and it is not difficult to see the weariness at a night full of wrong, earthquakes and executions representing something like Auden's own spiritual exhaustion in early 1939, carrying on only because 'like a sentinel, he could not sleep'. The same weariness can be found in many of the poems of *Another Time*: in the portrait of 'Matthew Arnold', 'a dark disordered city', his gift destroyed by filial piety and paternal solicitude but 'observant like a beggar' (the echo of 'Voltaire' suggesting a shared theme), or of 'A. E. Housman', the homosexual poet and scholar deliberately settling for the third-rate and the dry-as-dust, keeping 'tears like dirty postcards in a drawer', privately obsessed with 'Something to do with violence and the poor'. 'Brussels in Winter' sums up the demoralized *mise-en-scène* of all these poems: one in which only 'the homeless and the really humbled' seem sure of their place, and the traveller, killing time in the streets of a cold, unwelcoming city, buys brief succour from a prostitute.

Another trophy of Auden's visit to Brussels, 'Musée des Beaux Arts', extends the desolation to the realm of art, finding reflected in Breughel's canvases his own jaundiced view of the ubiquity, irrelevance and marginality of human suffering in an indifferent world. In these paintings, 'Everything turns

43

away | Quite leisurely from the disaster', as Auden himself must have felt the world had turned away from the miseries and atrocities of a low dishonest decade. In 'The Capital', the city is again a place of betrayal where 'lives are made for a temporary use' and the lonely are battered like pebbles.

This, too, is the spirit in which 'In Memory of W. B. Yeats' records the Irish poet's death in the dead of winter, amidst frozen brooks, deserted airports and statues disfigured by snow. The imagery is insistent and persuasive. In this killing time, whatever the time of day it is always frozen midnight. Not only was the day of Yeats's death 'a dark cold day'; by the end of the poem we have moved from dispirited afternoon to a Europe locked in 'the nightmare of the dark' and finally to 'the bottom of the night'. This is what the anti-Stalinist Communist Victor Serge, writing of this period, called 'the midnight of the century', and the ex-Stalinist Arthur Koestler (whom Auden met in Spain) summed up in the title of his novel of Communist disillusion as *Darkness at Noon* (1940).

Poem XXX of *Another Time*, which provides the volume's title, summarizes the causes of this disenchantment in terms which echo Koestler's. This is a world of fugitives who flee themselves in illusory loyalties to national or international banners, but who deep down, no longer wish to belong. For all their future-fatigue, however, they are still not ready to accept that 'It is to-day in which we live', not some imaginary elsewhere:

> So many try to say Not Now,
> So many have forgotten how
> To say I Am, and would be
> Lost, if they could, in history.

Such hopes for 'another time' bring not camaraderie but loneliness and self-loathing for having embraced lies. But in one sense this is already 'another time': that decade of credulous dishonesty is now over. As 'Our Bias' observes, time has patience for innumerable errors, revealing in the end the wrongness of always being right (which sounds like a jab at Communist certitudes, finally exposed as bankrupt by the Nazi–Soviet Pact). Unlike the lion and the rose, we cannot go 'straight to where we are' (the title's analogy is with bowling), because we lack their undeviating will to live. Where we are is Hell, 'Hell' suggests, echoing Marlowe's *Faustus*, though 'Hell is neither here nor there, | Hell is not anywhere', a limbo of unmeaning where time is killed as surely as in that phoney war which for almost a year haunted Europe's 'ruined century'. Contempt for all the past decade's shallow talk, prattling of posterity and lying to oneself, exhausting the dictionary without saying a true word, culminates in the miserable insight that, instead of averting, it has brought Hell into being.

'Law like Love' sees such concepts as 'Law' as mere rationalizations of competing self-interests, 'the clothes men wear | Anytime, anywhere'. Underlying all is a universal wish for non-involvement, to 'slip out of our own position | Into an unconcerned condition'. In this moral void, 'Victor', 'James Honeyman' and 'Miss Gee' turn in their private hells, the roistering ballad measures and mordant brutality of their cautionary tales à la Belloc underlining the message that their own accidie and self-absorption has caused their downfall. All love's bright hopes are soiled, as in 'As I walked out one evening', by a Time which like a disapproving (and interfering) voyeur 'watches from the shadow | And coughs when you would kiss'. The poem's chilling conclusion, that 'Life remains a blessing, | Although you cannot bless', adds insult to injury with a moral injunction that turns as it is uttered into something more like a curse: '"You shall love your crooked neighbour | With your crooked heart."'

The best one can expect in such a world is the fumbled embrace and momentary tenderness, 'Human on my faithless arm', of the one-night-stand in 'Lullaby', or the jaunty resignation, at the end of things, of 'Roman Wall Blues', which recovers a little equanimity by giving up on justifications: 'I'm a Wall soldier, I don't know why.' Here, like the homosexual Rimbaud, one becomes a poet only when 'the rhetorician's lie' bursts like a frozen pipe – an alarmingly negative view of art as a disabling disenchantment. Rimbaud's solution, the poem indicates, was to run away, and this seems to be how Auden saw his own position at the time. Even the supposedly joyous wedding hymn 'Epithalamion' with which the volume ends opens on a note of global war, as 'explosives blow to dust | Friends and hopes'; and it closes with what, like the end of 'September 1, 1939', seems a rather desperate attempt to kindle an affirming flame from negation and despair, finding bleak consolation in an art which sees Mozart 'Turning poverty to song', Goethe 'Placing every human wrong', and Wagner 'Organis[ing] his wish for death | Into a tremendous cry'.

Art, indeed, affords the sole positive note in a lugubrious volume, offering the calm faith that came to Herman Melville after all the shipwrecks of 'sensible success': 'Goodness existed: that was the new knowledge.' To persuade himself of the same, Auden in the Yeats elegy urged the poet to 'make a vineyard of the curse', converting 'human unsuccess' into 'a rapture of distress' through 'the farming of a verse'. At the end of his tether, the writer runs howling to his art, emulating that moment in the last line of 'Herman Melville' where the novelist 'sat down at his desk and wrote a story'.

MAKING NOTHING HAPPEN

First, however, the artist had to stand trial for social irresponsibility. Auden confided to Stephen Spender in 1964 that Yeats's poems made him 'whore after lies' and that Yeats had become for him 'a symbol of my own devil of unauthenticity...false emotions, inflated rhetoric, empty sonorities'.[2] 'In Memory of W. B. Yeats' makes the older poet a surrogate for Auden's own self-castigation, in language which extends the metaphor of judicial enquiry. So, too, does 'The Public v. the Late Mr William Butler Yeats', Auden's 1939 prose obituary in *Partisan Review*, cast as a trial in which a Public Prosecutor indicts Yeats's feudal mentality and fascist sympathies, while a Defence Counsel argues that he redeemed himself by creating 'verbal structures' which made 'personal excitement socially available'. Art, the Defence argues, transcends partisanship; 'a product of history, not a cause', it 'does not re-enter history as an effective agent'. It is a 'fallacious belief that art ever makes anything happen'. Nevertheless, in 'the field of language' the increasingly 'democratic style' of Yeats's later verse is 'the diction of a just man, and it is for this reason that just men will always recognise the author as a master' (*EA* 389–93).

When the poem claims, then, that 'poetry makes nothing happen', it seeks to exempt Auden's own art from what a later poem, 'Their Lonely Betters', would call 'responsibility for time'. But it is also rejecting Yeats's anxiety in 'The Man and the Echo' about the part his writing may have played in propagating political murder in Ireland: 'Did that play of mine send out | Certain men the English shot?' It is no accident that the Yeats elegy immediately follows 'Spain 1937', in a series of occasional poems which includes the Freud and Toller elegies, 'September 1, 1939' and 'Epithalamion'. What Auden addresses here is his own guilt in condoning 'the necessary murder'. He was 'silly' like Yeats. He is the one awaiting trial 'in the cell of himself', who is 'almost convinced of his freedom'. He wants to be the 'free man' taught to praise 'in the prison of his days'. He hopes that, like Yeats, Kipling, and Claudel, he too will be pardoned by Time for writing well. The image of 'the Just' flashing out their messages over a darkened earth at the end of 'September 1, 1939' expresses the same hope: that, like Yeats, he will be numbered among the 'just men' by a posterity which forgives the 'Intellectual disgrace' of his generation.

What this disgrace might be is indicated by a passage in *New Year Letter* addressed to Elizabeth Mayer, a mother-substitute, like him exiled in New York but, a German Lutheran married to a Jew, for more pressing reasons. In this, his first major American poem, Auden submits his own life and work to a summary tribunal where, as in the Yeats obituary, he is both prosecution and defence, and which, punningly, passes no sentences but his own. The intense interrogation to which he submits himself is twofold. His art is judged by a tribunal composed of the literary mentors he nominates. As befits the 'Double Man' of the American title poem, his eclectic list is made up of antinomies: Dante and Blake, Rimbaud and Dryden, Catullus and Tennyson, Baudelaire and Hardy, Rilke and Kipling. His literary 'crimes' are primarily 'slubber[ing] through | With slip and slapdash what I do' and adopting the 'preacher's loose immodest tone' – something he disowned but regularly practised. (The preacher's words, unlike the poet's, intend to make something happen.) The other trial is for a capital offence in the realm of history, for 'The situation of our time | Surrounds us like a baffling crime.'

The body on the carpet is not now, as in 'Detective Story', simply our personal happiness, but European Civilization itself.

Given its recent failures and its present collapse, it is something we all had grounds for loathing, which makes us all murder suspects. The detective who comes to solve the crime, however, turns out to be Hitler himself, 'one inspector dressed in brown' (a reference to the Nazi Brownshirts), his very madness making him the only consistent diagnostician of a distracted world. For his own reasons Hitler 'makes the murderer whom he pleases', bringing an end to the investigations. But indeed, the poem agrees, 'the guilt is everywhere', shared by all sides in the present conflict, in a million individual acts of commission and omission which boil down, in the statistician's calculations, to the gross behaviour of the group mind and 'average man':

> Upon each English conscience lie
> Two decades of hypocrisy,
> And not a German can be proud
> Of what his apathy allowed.

The present deluge of tyranny and force has a double origin: Plato's 'lie of intellect', that all are weak but the Elect Philosophers and must therefore be controlled by them in a strong centralized State, and Rousseau's 'falsehood of the flesh', that men are born free but are everywhere in social chains. The same antithesis contrasts the lie of Authority with that of the sensual man-in-the-street in 'September 1, 1939'. This 'social lie' appears double, but our 'political distress' has a single source in our divided nature, which misreads the dialectic of freedom and necessity, sundering individual from society, and inviting us to join the great fascist retreat.

Two devils preside over *New Year Letter*. One is the tempter who invites the disillusioned idealist and Simon-pure utopian to throw out the baby with the bathwater, rejecting his cherished beliefs in socialism and the possibility of a just society reconciled with individual liberty, simply because one system in which he placed undue faith has shown itself to be bankrupt. Another poetic surrogate, Wordsworth, had made a similar mistake in falling for the libertarian rhetoric of the French Revolution, expecting the Millenium to be delivered by what was no more than a provisional regime, only to be bitterly disabused, as the devil knew he would be, into the contrary error, ending his life an old Tory supporting the Congress of Vienna, the established

Church and Squirearchy. This devil does not tell lies so much as half-truths, which 'the gift of double-focus', provided by the magic lamp of art, enables us to deconstruct. *New Year Letter* admits that 'Art is not life, and cannot be | A midwife to society'. But, if art makes nothing happen, its very duplicity can be a virtue. As one of the notes to the poem asserts: 'All knowledge that conflicts with itself is Poetic Fiction.' This Blakean double vision is presided over by a second, more benign devil: for 'The Devil, indeed, is the father of Poetry, for poetry might be defined as the clear expression of mixed feelings. The Poetic mood is never indicative.'[3] 'Poetry' here, as in Greek *poesis*, means any kind of artistic making. It is actually music that makes the running in *New Year Letter*, from the street singing with which it opens on New Year's Eve 1939, through Buxtehude's baroque passacaglias, converting street music into 'a civitas of sound', to the Schubert, Mozart and Gluck at Elizabeth Mayer's dinner party, representing that 'real republic' to which all politics aspires; and not excluding on the way even Isolde's *Liebestod*, summoned by a devil who wants to tempt us with the death wish. Such models of harmony, reconciling order and freedom, become the imaginary utopias against which to measure a world at war, icons of what might be involved in building the Just City, prefiguring 'The "Nowhere-without-No" that is | The justice of societies' at a time when news is seldom good. Making nothing happen, it seems, can have a utopian double focus.

CLERKISH TREASONS

It was, significantly, the American writer Herman Melville who provided Auden's first exemplar of this new dispensation. A little later, in 1941, another American 'Master of nuance and scruple' was called upon to intercede 'For the treason of all clerks' in 'At the Grave of Henry James'. Auden's phrase had been coined by the French writer Julien Benda in a celebrated book, *La Trahison des clercs* (1927), which argued that modern artists and intellectuals had betrayed the disinterestedness of their calling by dabbling in politics, sullying the eternal values of the intellect with the partisan and ephemeral allegiances of left and right. This was to become the grace note of Auden's writing

49

W. H. AUDEN and CHESTER KALLMAN in Venice, 1949

in the coming decades. His 1964 retrospect 'The Cave of Making', dedicated to the memory of MacNeice and reflecting on the 'unpopular art' they shared, speaks of a time when 'any faith, if we had it, in immanent virtue died', and adds, carefully:

> More than ever
> life-out-there is goodly, miraculous, lovable,
> but we shan't, not since Stalin and Hitler,
> trust ourselves ever again: we know that, subjectively,
> all is possible.

Auden's own clerkish treason was perceived rather differently at the time. It is difficult to think back into the outrage and denunciation which accompanied his and Isherwood's emigration to the United States just as war broke out. It was even proposed in the House of Commons that, as 'British citizens of military age', they be 'summoned back for registration and calling up'.[4] Justifying his decision in a letter to Spender in 1941, Auden insisted that 'the intellectual warfare goes on always and everywhere, and no one has a right to say that this place or that time is where all intellectuals ought to be'.[5] A few years earlier, reviewing *Journey to a War*, the American Lincoln Kirstein had put his finger on what such 'treachery' really entailed, calling Auden 'a really dangerous person' because 'he threatens even our most recent and difficultly intrenched ideas', practising 'pragmatic treachery to every preconceived poetic formula', recruiting as 'forced allies' every poet from Beowulf to Byron, and then scrapping them as soon as it suited him in order to 'found a new front which may have certain special uses'.[6]

What was needed in 1939 was not so much 'another time' as another place in which to open a second front, where poetry might again be possible. Auden and Isherwood arrived in New York at the end of January 1939. In April Auden met Chester Kallman, the 18-year-old student at Brooklyn College who was shortly to become, despite periods of bitter resentment, his lifelong lover and companion. (Dorothy Farnan, Kallman's father's second wife, has described this relationship at length.) In exile, in a dark time, Auden had, it appeared, come home to love. Before long he had opted to become what he was to call a 'metic', a resident alien, in New York. In 1946 he completed his naturalization process and became an American citizen.

Auden would later write of the contrast between the United States and Europe, in his Introduction to an anthology of modern American poetry:

> In a land which is fully settled, most men must accept their local environment or try to change it by political means; only the exceptionally gifted or adventurous can leave to seek his fortune elsewhere.
>
> In America, on the other hand, to move on and make a fresh start somewhere else is still the normal reaction to dissatisfaction or failure. Such social fluidity has important psychological effects. Since movement involves breaking social and personal ties, the habit creates an attitude towards personal relationships in which impermanence is taken for granted.

This new elsewhere is a projection in space, not time, not a dispossessing future but a liberating displacement, offering what a Thirties poem spoke of as 'New styles of architecture, a change of heart' figured in the skyscrapers which affirm the strength of Collective Man: 'To be able at any time to break with the past, to move and keep on moving lessens the significance not only of the past but also of the future which is reduced to the immediate future, and minimises the importance of political action.'[7]

Certainly America witnessed Auden's own rapid disengagement from politics. In an unpublished essay written in the summer of 1939 he revealed that, though he still believed in socialism, the artists who in 1931 took up politics as 'an exciting new subject' needed, if they were not to ruin themselves or harm the causes they espoused, to reconsider their position:

> As far as the course of political events is concerned they might just as well have done nothing.... The artist qua artist is no reformer. Slums, war, disease are part of his material, and as such he loves them. The writers who, like Hemingway and Malraux, really profited as writers from the Spanish Civil War, and were perhaps really some practical use as well, had the time of their lives there.
>
> The voice of the Tempter: 'Unless you take part in the class struggle, you cannot become a major writer.'[8]

Whether Auden became quite the blue-eyed unpolitical innocent he claimed is another question. In the Faber anthology he was not ashamed to admit to stylistic opportunism, noting that 'The social strains which later break out in political action are first experienced by artists as a feeling that the current modes of expression are no longer capable of dealing with their real concerns.'[9] The forms he deploys in the long poems of the 1940s all foreground their elaboration and artifice in addressing a world that seems incorrigibly stagey and unreal. The first, styling itself a 'Christmas Oratorio', deploys the self-conscious devices of chorus, semi-chorus and fugal chorus, repetition, counterpoint and recitative, and all the emblematic figures of the Nativity story, including a Star which gets its own singing part, as well as a Narrator and a public apologia by Herod in the terms of an up-to-date, hard-boiled broadcast by a well-meaning but embattled politician. The second, a 'Commentary' on *The Tempest*, is a second-order reprise of the characters of Shakespeare's most self-consciously artificial and theatrical play, in which each gets to offer some kind of lyric or meditative *apologia pro vita sua*. The third defines itself as a 'Baroque Eclogue', doubly artificial, and deploys all the devices of allegory, masque and obsessive wordplay to underline its unreality.

A directly personal grief adds its intensity to the spiritual dryness of these wartime writings. In 1941 a telegram informed Auden of his mother's death. His desolation was deepened because the news came at a time when the relationship with Kallman had broken down, possibly irreparably. 'For the Time Being', which he dedicated to his mother's memory, convinced of his own treason in the face of highest obligations, submitted his past life to the exacting scrutiny of that ultimate stranger, death. 'The Sea and the Mirror', the other work in this volume, describes a posthumous world, set for ever in the aftermath of action, that stillness after the play ends when all the characters have been assigned their true places, and all that remains is a moment to reflect on what it all signified. But it is also that place of anxious, provisional and temporary being from which *For the Time Being* and *The Age of Anxiety* begin.

Auden had written in 1943 that 'Art ... is not Magic, i.e., a means by which the artist communicates or arouses his feelings in others, but a mirror in which they may become conscious of what their own feelings really are: its proper effect, in fact, is disenchanting'.[10] This is the function of the mirror held up to the flux of reality in 'The Sea and the Mirror', rejecting Prospero's manipulative magic in the name of a true, disenchanted seeing. Prospero, addressing Ariel as the figure of his art, has finally discovered that his magic is 'the power to enchant | That comes from disillusion'. Yet art's echo and mirror can still overcome the bestiality of Caliban's carnal world, where 'most desires end up in stinking ponds'.

At the end of 'For the Time Being', Mary and Joseph have to enter the mirror 'No authority can pass' in their flight into Egypt, and pass through a desert full of echoes where 'the weather-glass | Is set at Alas' (recalling History's verdict in *Spain*), 'everyone goes to pieces', 'anguish arrives by cable', and 'it's always three in the morning'. Only thus 'our future may be freed from our past' and 'our death' transformed by 'the new life'. Similarly, in *The Age of Anxiety*, the middle-aged, disillusioned homosexual Malin speaks of staggering drunkenly to the bathroom mirror 'To meet one's madness, when what mother said seems | Such darling rubbish', and the decent advice of the liberal weeklies is useless. Clearly, the desire for 'Our death, death of the old gang' of the early poetry is still strong. But now the true elsewhere by which quotidian reality is to be judged is no longer of this world, and art and religion may conspire to give us access.

NEGATIVE KNOWLEDGES

Auden's explanation of what Ariel and Prospero signify is fairly straightforward:

> [W]e want a poem to be a beautiful object, a verbal Garden of Eden which, by its formal perfection, keeps alive in us the hope that there exists a state of joy without evil or suffering which it can and should be our destiny to attain. At the same time, we look to a poem for some kind of illumination about our present wandering condition, since, without self-insight and knowledge of the world, we must err blindly with little chance of realizing our hope.... [I]n every poet, there dwells an Ariel, who sings, and a Prospero, who comprehends, but in any particular poem ... one of the partners plays a greater role than the other.[11]

This is an old distinction, as an essay on Robert Frost reveals, arguing that 'Art arises out of our desire for both beauty and truth and our knowledge that they are not identical', so that 'every poem shows some sign of a rivalry between Ariel and

Prospero; in every good poem their relation is more or less happy, but it is never without its tensions'. Tension lies in the conflict between our desire for the poem to be 'a verbal earthly paradise, a timeless world of pure play', which delights 'precisely because of its contrast to our historical existence with all its insoluble problems and inescapable suffering', and our wish for it to be 'true', and to provide 'some kind of revelation of what life is really like and free us from self-enchantment and deception' (DH 337–8).

Prospero takes on a rather more problematic, personal significance in 'Balaam and His Ass'. This essay sees *The Tempest* as a 'disquieting work', for, whereas in all the other late comedies, ' "Pardon's the word to all" ', in this play 'both the repentance of the guilty and the pardon of the injured seem more formal than real', while 'Prospero's forgiving is more the contemptuous pardon of a man who knows that he has his enemies completely at his mercy than a heartfelt reconciliation'. Prospero 'has the coldness of someone who has come to the conclusion that human nature is not worth very much, that human relations are, at their best, pretty sorry affairs'. Various contemporary poems suggest the opinion is Auden's own. But Prospero differs from Auden in one key particular: 'it never occurs to him that he, too, might have erred and be in need of pardon' (DH 128–30).

The subject, for Auden, is a shifting ratio of Prospero, Ariel and Caliban, ego, imagination and instinct: 'As a biological organism Man is a natural creature subject to the necessities of nature; as a being with a consciousness and will, he is at the same time a historical person with the freedom of the spirit' (DH 130). We can never really know our nature because the act of knowing 'is itself a spiritual and historical act', not an absolute state. We can only be known, and our temporal anxiety arises from the knowledge that, in being known, we are also seen through. This is 'the Horror' that in 'For the Time Being' starts to scratch its way into our lives:

> We can only say that now It is there and that nothing
> We learnt before It was there is now of the slightest use,
> For nothing like It has happened before.

As in Eliot's *Four Quartets*, whose cadences are recalled here, the Annunciation for Auden makes an unconditional claim, calls our whole being into question, disclosing

> that although there's a person we know all about
> Still bearing our name and loving himself as before,
> That person has become a fiction; our true existence
> Is decided by no one and has no importance to love.

Such a revelation must be faced with neither despair nor the child's blind faith, but with a mature bitter recognition that there is 'nowhere that is not a desert' and no 'magic secret of how to extemporize life'. 'Advent' announces that 'As long as the self can say "I", it is impossible not to rebel, and the miracle cannot occur.' The phrasing is picked up elsewhere in the poem, in 'The Meditation of Simeon', which insists that 'our redemption is no longer a question of pursuit but of surrender to Him who is always and everywhere present', in the hope that 'we may depart from our anxiety into His peace'. Such 'temporizing' is figured in the title's play on words: thinking it is only temporary, we kill the time which is the only time we have as beings. But this temporizing empty *durée* can be transformed in the perspective of Messianic time into the ontological, full time of Being discussed by such philosophers as Heidegger:

> For all societies and epochs are transient details
> Transmitting an everlasting opportunity
> That the Kingdom of Heaven may come, not in our present
> And not in our future, but in the Fullness of Time.

In this sense 'The Time Being is ... the most trying time of all', a time where we are perpetually on trial. Auden here extends into a metaphysical dimension the judicial imagery of his earlier reflections on art and life. 'He is the Truth', the oratorio concludes, 'Seek Him in the Kingdom of Anxiety'. This is the task of his next volume, which develops the idea of life as a Kafkaesque mixture of trial and quest. 'We belong to our kind, | Are judged as we judge', reflects the well-meaning and ineffectual Malin, Auden's surrogate, at the end of *The Age of Anxiety*: 'It is where we are wounded, that is when He speaks.'

In a review just before he began the poem, Auden defined the 'basic human problem' as 'man's anxiety in time; e.g. his present anxiety over himself in relation to his past and his parents (Freud), his present anxiety over himself in relation to his future and his neighbours (Marx), his present anxiety over himself in relation to eternity and God (Kierkegaard)'.[12] *The Age of Anxiety* records the impotence of individuals reduced to generic ciphers, massacred in nameless multitudes by a global world war that has become a cosmic force. Its elaborate allegorical framework allows Auden to explore the manifestation of this anxiety at physical, socio-economic, psychological and spiritual levels, in the overlaid orders of nature, society, personal life and metaphysics.

Four strangers, three men and a woman, are brought together in a New York bar on All Souls' Night by the news bulletin of beach-heads, battles and negotiations, speaking of a shared world of grief and loss where, in the words of the refrain that links their separate reminiscences, 'Many have perished; more will.' In 'The Seven Ages' each recounts a different version of Shakespeare's ages of man. They undertake in 'The Seven Stages' a tipsy tour of an allegorical landscape likened to the material body, and come, finally, to a paralysing disenchantment:

> Graven on all things...
> Is the same symbol, the signature
> Of reluctant allegiance to a lost cause.

'The Dirge' mourns this lost cause as an imaginary father figure, 'some semi-divine stranger with superhuman powers', Gilgamesh, Napoleon, Solon or Sherlock Holmes (Stalin could easily join the list) 'who, long or lately, has always died or disappeared'. Now that they know 'Our lost dad, | Our colossal father' is dead, leaving no one to dust 'the cobwebbed kingdoms', the disenchanted wanderers retire to the woman Rosetta's apartment for a late-night binge, each secretly resolving 'to banish such gloomy reflections and become, or at least appear, carefree and cheerful.'

The distinction between becoming and appearing recalls Reinhold Niebuhr's *The Nature and Destiny of Man*, the first volume of which Auden had reviewed in 1941, which elucidates the poem's title and theology:

Man, being both free and bound, both limited and limitless, is anxious. Anxiety is the inevitable concomitant of the paradox of freedom and finiteness in which man is involved. Anxiety is the internal precondition of sin. It is the inevitable spiritual state of man.[13]

As the young sailor's name, Emble, seems a truncated emblem, so the name of the Irish shipping clerk, Quant, reminds us of that fallen world of matter ruled by quantum physics, in which the atom bomb had recently been dropped on Japan. Malin's conclusion that 'For the others, like me, there is only the flash | Of negative knowledge' recalls with a *frisson* that annihilating nuclear brightness. But this 'negative knowledge' is also the *Via Negativa* of spiritual insight explored recently in Eliot's *Four Quartets*, the route to what Malin calls 'That Always-Opposite which is the whole subject | Of our not-knowing'. Through the idea of the 'quantum leap' the poem subverts a murderous physics with a metaphysics of redemption, turning it into that Kierkegaardian leap into commitment which creates a new meaning and knowledge *ex nihilo*, transforming dread. For Auden, this leap reiterates that in which the Oedipal infant submits to the Name of the Father:

> The gulf before him with guilt beyond,
> Whatever that is, whatever why
> Forbids his bound; till that ban tempts him;
> He jumps and is judged: he joins mankind,
> The fallen families, freedom lost,
> Love become Law.

For Malin, 'The police, | The dress-designers, etc., | Who manage the mirrors' construct a stage upon which we delude ourselves with an illusion of meaning, finding 'The same | Old treatments for tedium vitae, | Religion, Politics, Love'. In 'The Sea and the Mirror' existence was a conjuror's routine of mirrors and wire in a world where no 'authority gives | Existence its surprise'. In 'For the Time Being' Christmas's cardboard and tinsel miracle was put together at the beginning and dismantled at the end. The 'seven stages' through which the body passes in *The Age of Anxiety* are also theatrical stages on which the self struts and frets its hour. But this theatricality, which had previously suggested that human life is a sham, becomes here the improbable ground of redemption. The world-weary, middle-aged narrator of *The Age of Anxiety* concludes that, to live in this world, we have to invent a dramatic *persona* for which we then assume responsibility, becoming a subject by pretending to be one:

only animals who are below civilization and the angels who are beyond it can be sincere. Human beings are, necessarily, actors who cannot become something before they have first pretended to be it; and they can be divided, not into the hypocritical and the sincere, but into the sane who know they are acting and the mad who do not.

This is the stage set for the poetry of the next two decades.

4

The Inconstant Ones

THE SUBURB OF DISSENT

In 1939 Auden's decision to settle in the United States had seemed to fix on some final frame of reference from which to consider the contemporary world. In renouncing England, however, he was seeking not a place to put down but, on the contrary, one in which to 'live deliberately without roots'.[1] The imagery of passing-through pervades his post-war volumes, whether the Irish transit lounge of 'Air Port' in *Nones* (1951) – later retitled with even greater insistence 'In Transit' – or the through-train of 'A Permanent Way' in *The Shield of Achilles* (1955), which permits the luxury of daydreaming about settling in places where one knows the train doesn't stop. As the title suggests, the train symbolizes the kind of provisional permanence which is all Auden thought possible for mortal creatures (and all he desired). The 'mixed feelings' of all these volumes are signalled by 'In Praise of Limestone', the second poem in *Nones*, which turns the limestone landscapes of his childhood into a *paysage moralisé* of the modern condition:

> If it form the one landscape that we the inconstant ones
>   Are consistently homesick for, this is chiefly
> Because it dissolves in water.

There is a kind of metaphysical punning in that dissoluteness and inconstancy, recalling the 'water | Running away in the dark' which had woken the 'Secret Agent' in 1928 to his own mortal insecurity. Landscapes of granite or gravel may summon potential Saints and Caesars to their destinies and the ocean call the reckless to the solitude and death that frees them. But this limestone landscape is not itself 'the sweet home that it

60

looks, | Nor its peace the historical calm of a site | Where something was settled once and for all'. Nothing is settled in a landscape whose primary dimension is not space (as it would be in America) but time, embodying a storied antiquity which, though here clearly Italian, recalls such English locations of his youth as the moors near Hadrian's Wall of *New Year Letter*. These became, by association with the felicitously named river Eden, a symbol of the 'original address' from which 'Man faulted into consciousness', thereby founding civil life. We are not surprised, then, that 'In Praise of Limestone' ends with the same geo/theological pun, asserting that such a landscape remains the nearest this poet at least can get to imagining 'a faultless love | Or the life to come'.

In the house at 7 Middagh Street in New York's Brooklyn Heights which he rented along with an assortment of other literati and oddballs (including the stripper Gipsy Rose Lee), Auden found the kind of casual bohemian ethos which promised just such a gratifyingly permanent impermanency in the (real) life to come. In case, however, the conventions of domesticity conspired to make even this provisional refuge, and its successor apartments, assume the furniture of home, and just as he had taken on US citizenship, he and Kallman began to spend half of each year in Europe, between 1947 and 1957 on the Italian island of Ischia, near Capri, and from then until Auden's death in 1973 at Kirchstetten, a small village in Lower Austria 40 kilometres from Vienna. In addition, between 1956 and 1961 he visited Oxford regularly as its elected Professor of Poetry, and during 1972–3 occasionally occupied a cottage in the grounds of Christ Church, his old college. (His reflections on the changes his *alma mater* had undergone are presented, veiled as a vision of Bohemia, in 'Forty Years On'.)

The plane journey of another poem in *The Shield of Achilles*, 'Ode to Gaea', explains the virtue of such intercontinental peregrinations. The view of post-war Europe the plane affords puts the political and cultural divisions of the planet in humbling perspective. Gaea, mother earth, is indifferent to which 'sub-species of folly' pertains to the 'pretty molehills' below or where on the 'pocket-handkerchief of a plain | the syntax changes', and in 'this new culture of the air' it is possible to feel the airy hauteur of view indicated by the demeaning nouns. Auden's Airman, in middle age a jet-setting sceptic, risks the hubris of Gulliver among the Lilliputians, but we share his amusement at the parochial loyalties of his fellow traveller, a tired old diplomat embarrassed because he doesn't know whether to smile on the territory below because it belongs to '"our great good ally"', or scowl because it's part of an unnamed Soviet Union's '"vast and detestable empire"'.

Auden may have shed his ultra-left allegiances of the 1930s; but not simply to adopt an alternative set of prejudices like those former Communists who turned Nato intellectuals during the worst days of the Cold War.[2] The dedicatory poem of *Nones*, to the Christian socialists Reinhold and Ursula Niebuhr, laments an era in which 'All words like peace and love, | All sane affirmative speech' have been 'soiled, profaned, debased' by rival political camps. From the late 1940s onwards on both sides of the Iron Curtain the confrontation of the world's new superpowers, USA and USSR, had co-opted such concepts as 'peace' and 'love' to the 'horrid mechanical screech' of their rival propaganda machines, the McCarthy witch-hunts in the United States matching the show trials in Eastern Europe. (In 'Whitsunday in Kirchstetten' Auden drolly dubs the Soviet Union 'peace-loving Crimtartary'.)

Niebuhr's book *The Irony of American History*, based on lecture series given in 1949 and 1951, had interpreted the Cold War, and its corrosive effects on American society, from a 'critical, but not hostile, detachment' in the light of a 'Christian faith [which] tends to make the ironic view of human evil in history the normative one'.[3] Echoing Niebuhr, the dedication to *Nones* concludes that the only uncompromised civil style that remains is 'the wry, the sotto voce, | Ironic and monochrome' still practised in 'the suburb of dissent'. If, in the words of 'Journey to Iceland', 'Our time has no favourite suburb', the ironic, relativist perspectives of Auden's post-war collections offer a view from the margins of that new world order he had described in 1951:

> To all of us...in the middle of the twentieth century, the Roman Empire is like a mirror in which we see reflected the brutal, vulgar, powerful yet despairing image of our own technological civilization, an imperium which now covers the entire globe, for all nations, capitalist, socialist and communist, are united in their worship of

mass, technique and temporal power. What fascinates and terrifies us about the Roman Empire is not that it finally went smash, but that, away from the start, it managed to last for five centuries without creativity, warmth or hope.[4]

This is more wide-reaching than mere US dominance of the post-war world. Rather it is what the essay 'The Poet and the City' (*DH*, 72–89) describes as a wholly new order of things where 'Technology, with its ever accelerating transformation of man's way of living, has made it impossible for us to imagine what life will be like even twenty years from now.' A dehumanizing and increasingly totalitarian global technocracy had produced a new ruling class east and west, 'the Management', living in an 'official world [with] the smell of an unreality in which persons are treated as statistics'. What this new manageriat manages is 'the Public', defined by Kierkegaard, he says, as ' "an abstract and deserted void which is everything and nothing" '. An inert collectivity of passive consumers manipulated by the new mass media, the Public is, unlike Shakespeare's crowd, 'odorless', but it occasionally embodies itself in the kind of mob that gathers for any spectacle offering 'yet another proof that physical force is the Prince of this world against whom no love of the heart shall prevail'.

This public is the 'faceless many' rubber-necking the Crucifixion in 'Nones', guaranteed to 'Collect when any world is to be wrecked, | Blown up, burnt down, cracked open, | Felled, sawn in two, hacked through, torn apart'. Such, also, is that 'crowd of ordinary decent folk' which, in the title poem of *The Shield of Achilles*, 'Watched from without but neither moved nor spoke' at a public execution (whether of criminals, partisans or enemy soldiers is of no importance) which, for all the secular trappings of a Nazi or Stalinist atrocity, recalls the Crucifixion of Christ.

Auden was probably influenced in his reading of modern industrial society by the critique made by the American radical C. Wright Mills in *The New Men of Power* in 1948.[5] Certainly 'The Managers', written the same year, seems to recall Wright Mills's famous image of a contemporary reality organized at all levels by the 'managers of discontent':

> The last word on how we may live or die
> Rests today with such quiet
> Men, working too hard in rooms that are too big,

Reducing to figures
What is the matter, what is to be done.

The awesome power of this new class had been enhanced by the time Auden wrote by Soviet acquisition of the atom bomb, thanks in part to the clerkish treason of his one-time friend Guy Burgess, at that moment still an undiscovered Russian mole in the Foreign Office. In 'Whitsunday in Kirchstetten' in 1966 Auden was to recall the Soviet President Krushchev's threat to the West at the UN General Assembly: 'We shall bury you | and dance at the wake.' In 'The Managers', Lenin's phrase 'what is to be done', which Auden had relished in the 1930s for its promise of the surgeon's scalpel, has become a threat of annihilation wielded by the Managers east and west alike. Managers need to be reminded, he now wrote, 'that the managed are people with faces, not anonymous numbers' (*DH* 88). Once the Managers perceive the managed as the problem ('what is the matter'), it is a short step to solving it by reducing them to mere matter, as Hiroshima and Nagasaki had shown.

Auden returned to the theme of nuclear catastrophe in most of his post-war volumes. In 'Thanksgiving for a Habitat' in *About the House* (1965) he fears being translated 'at the nod | of some jittery commander...in a nano-second | to a c.c. of poisonous nothing | in a giga-death', and the language itself apes the Managers' own dehumanized rhetoric. In *City Without Walls* (1969) he girns in 'Ode to Terminus' (the god of final things) at the 'High Priests of telescopes and cyclotrons' and 'the sacrilegious technocrat' whose colossal immodesty has 'plundered and poisoned' the planet, and in 'Prologue at Sixty' at the sophisticated weapon systems of 'our sorry conceited O' (an ironic travesty of Shakespeare's famous image) which could well complete the process. The title poem of *Epistle to a Godson* (1972) renames the Managers as 'our global Archons' (the chief magistrates of ancient Athens), whose scientists, like 'clever little boys' have built devices for the potentially lethal disassembling of matter. In *Thank You, Fog* (1974), 'Address to the Beasts' contrasts those creatures which have to take lives to live but 'never kill for applause' with our own lapsed humanity which, by its own folly, 'one balmy day...might well become, | not fossils, but vapour'. Human inconstancy was now compounded by the threat of species extinction.

GOING SMASH

'Physics, geology and biology have now replaced this everlasting universe with a picture of nature as a process in which nothing is now what it was or what it will be', Auden wrote in 'The Poet and the City', finding his own sense of impermanence writ large in the cosmos: 'Today, Christian and Atheist alike are eschatologically minded', so that, with 'no model of endurance to go by', the modern artist is tempted to abandon the search for perfection 'and be content with sketches and improvisation' (*DH* 78). Such an outcome had implications for Auden's poetry at the level of both ideas and form. 'A Walk After Dark', which concludes *Nones*, takes consolation in the clockwork spectacle of a star-spangled universe middle-aged like himself, where 'the red pre-Cambrian light' of an aeon before the emergence of multicellular life is 'gone like Imperial Rome | Or myself at seventeen'. He speculates that even now some unknown event at the far end of the universe may have started a process which will end in the overthrow of all the laws that shape 'Our post-diluvian world'. If Imperial Rome has disappeared in the same blink of eternity as his shameful and shocking adolescence (and the elders it shocked), some such cosmic event may already have cast judgement on the middle age of 'My person, all my friends, | And these United States'.

This post-war poetry inhabits a world like that the modern Greek poet Cavafy discerned, according to Auden, in the long Indian summer of the Roman Empire. Like this other homosexual poet, Auden sought to offer 'exceptionally honest' witness to an order where the individual is 'politically power-less, and...politics are regarded with cynical amusement'. In the modern world, the Soviet Union's satellites and the United States' allies reproduce an ancient precedent: 'Officially, the satellite kingdoms are self-governing, but everyone knows that the rulers are puppets of Rome', so that their subjects ask 'why should they care what name their master bears?', and seek instead a merely personal fulfilment in an 'erotic world...of casual pickups and short-lived affairs', or in a Christianity whose 'principal concern was elsewhere'.[6]

Such a privatized erotic prospect lies behind the image of the 'nude young male' lounging against a rock 'displaying his dildo' which opens 'In Praise of Limestone', as it does the promise of a visit from the US Navy in the poem 'Fleet Visit'. The geopolitical situation nevertheless fills the public background of such private pleasures. The young men set down 'in this unamerican place', 'Fleet Visit' tells us, 'are not here because, | But only just-in-case'. In 1948 (as thereafter) the US Mediterranean Fleet had been mobilized in a show of strength 'just in case' the Italian Communists came to power in the first free elections for three decades. In 1951 the deliberately lower-case 'unamerican' downgrades the standing of Senator Joe McCarthy's House Committee on Unamerican Activities.[7] Auden, as a newly naturalized US citizen with a fellow-travelling past, had some cause for anxiety. One other prospective visitor to his house on Ischia in May that year was the defecting spy Guy Burgess, rumours of which led to the place being staked out by British Intelligence and the *Daily Express*.[8]

Perhaps Auden had this dandified Communist homosexual in mind when the previous year, with ponderously defensive playfulness, he had called an essay on Oscar Wilde 'A Playboy of the Western World, St Oscar, the Homintern Martyr', using Cyril Connolly's coinage (punning on 'Comintern', the shorthand for Communist International) as if to disarm in advance the insinuations Burgess was about to bring uncomfortably close to home. The essay speaks of modern intellectuals as 'incapable of understanding the role of power in society', because they occupy 'a social position which, like that of the gypsies, is interstitial' and thus 'prevents their having a subjective understanding of social and economic conditions'.[9]

This is that 'average elsewhereishness' which, in *About the House*, is somewhat dismissively identified in 'A Change of Air' as a kind of personal poetic bolt-hole. Auden's immediate post-war poetry, however, continued to find in such interstitiality, 'on the frontier', a point of vantage which, in the words of 'In Praise of Limestone', 'calls into question | All the Great Powers assume', in a phrase which fuses the world's dominant states with the whole secular order of things.

One of the earliest Italian poems, 'The Fall of Rome' (1947), still seems (in the terms of a famous Cavafy poem) to be 'waiting for the barbarians', gleefully overlaying the fall of the Roman Empire with contemporary images of social, economic and political collapse. For the Managers, the real end of such an order is signalled not by the noisy mutiny of unpaid Marines but by the quiet internal defection, somewhat like Burgess's, of the clerk who 'Writes I DO NOT LIKE MY WORK | On a pink official form'. The concluding lines still frame these last days with the 'Altogether elsewhere' of Northern tundras from which an earlier breed of barbarians erupted. But the vast herds of reindeer moving 'Silently and very fast' with which the poem closes, like the little birds on their nests eyeing 'each flu-infected city', call up an image not of bloodthirsty avengers but of a reproachful and outlasting natural innocence against which to judge human folly.

Similar points are made by other poems in *Nones* such as 'Their Lonely Betters' and 'Song' ('Deftly, admiral...'), which returns to the image of barbarian invasions only to heighten the sense of personal catastrophe in its final stanza. 'Under Sirius' appears to eschew apocalyptic yearnings (for some sudden and astonishing earthquake, for the descent of the Holy Ghost to 'translate the slipshod gathering') in the name of the present day's becalmed insipidity, in which the legion's spears grow rusty. But the poem maintains a delicate balance, as well it might in 1949, a year of apocalyptic 'translations' elsewhere as Mao Tse Tung's Red Army, which Auden had visited with Isherwood a decade earlier, swept to power throughout China. The poem warns its addressee Fortunatus, a poetaster bishop of Poitiers at the end of the Dark Ages (at the very moment that the barbarian invasions of Europe came to an end), that it is all very well dreaming of some Second Coming in which (a dig at Eliot's *Four Quartets*) 'all in the end shall be well'; providing one is not found wanting by the challenge of the Pantocrator Christ, '"Who are you and why?"'

Apocalyptic fantasies may give way in that final day to regret for 'these dull dog-days | Between event', which might in retrospect 'seem crowned with olive | And golden with self-praise'. The poem in some part shares Fortunatus' romantic millenarianism, but tempers it with a wise conservative caution about the fragility of peace and civilized order. This mood is far from complacency at the status quo: as 'A Walk After Dark' concludes, nothing has really changed: 'the present stalks abroad | Like the past and its wronged again | Whimper and are ignored.... | What needn't have happened did.'

Auden had had enough evidence since 1 September, 1939 of how easily Enlightenment could be driven away. In 1945 he had returned to Europe in US Airforce uniform to report on the effects of Allied bombing on civilian morale in Germany. He was appalled by what he saw, and this and the onset of the Cold War, dropping an Iron Curtain across the heart of the continent, gave rise to another 1949 poem. In the year of Berlin Blockade and Airlift, the melancholy but finally transcending spiritual vision of 'Memorial for the City' was dedicated to the recently deceased writer and amateur theologian Charles Williams, who had been the agent of Auden's return to Christianity.

The poem opens with what seems like an explicit repudiation of some characteristic Thirties positions, asserting that 'The eyes of the crow and the eye of the camera open | Onto Homer's world, not ours.' If the second image rejects Isherwood's claim to objective reportage in 'A Berlin Diary', 'I am a camera', the first disowns Auden's own 1930s appeal to 'Consider this... | As the hawk sees it or the helmeted airman'. Bird of prey has shrunk here to a carrion creature, and heroic airman to the war criminal whose bombing raids have reduced Europe's cities to ruins 'Where our past is a chaos of graves and the barbed-wire stretches ahead | Into our future till it is lost to sight'. This becomes for Auden the embodied landscape of a metaphysical condition. This is not Homer's world. 'Our grief is not Greek' because, unlike those pagans whose supreme deity was an indifferent mother earth, in the Christian era 'We know without knowing there is reason for what we bear, | That our hurt is not a desertion...'. Crow and camera lie because they 'Record a space where time has no place', in which all that one can say of endless catastrophe is 'That is the way things happen; for ever and ever...there is no one to blame.'

Increasingly, 'Elsewhere' seems to represent an other-worldly order of things set in disinterested judgement on our fallen sublunary world. 'A Change of Air' was to observe in terms recalling Eliot's *Four Quartets* that 'To go Elsewhere is to withdraw from movement', finding a 'healing disregard'. Such a perspective is quite distinct from the indifference with which the camera records history. In Auden's new, Christian eschatology the historical sense requires that we share the anxious faith of St Augustine (writing his *City of God* in the aftermath of the Goths' sack of Rome) in that true city which will rise again in judgement on the falsities, photographers, speeches, and statistics of the modern 'Metropolis, that too-great city'.

As a concerted Christian meditation on the human condition, 'Memorial for the City' is a *tour de force*. Yet it rises to greatness only in its negative moments, as, for example, in the third section's description of a divided world that looks all too like the desolation of contemporary Europe. Nevertheless, Auden never espoused a simple philosophy of *contemptus mundi*. His post-war volumes translate the political chiliasm of the 1930s into a much more chilling message: about that poisoning of the planet which in the last few years of this century has become central to any image of the future.

The Shield of Achilles opens with what sounds like an emphatically secular, even pagan sequence. Nevertheless, the light-hearted pastoral scenes of 'Bucolics' are from the start implicated in and subverted by fundamental questions of geopolitical power. 'Winds' opens the volume with the very thing it strives to renounce in plunging 'Deep below our violences', before going on to contrast a fallen Metropolis with an imagined 'Authentic City'. It is the 'darker map' of violence which invests this volume, most powerfully in its central, title poem. This contrasts the idyllic images of civic peace and harmony Thetis wants Hephaestos to depict on the shield he makes for her son, the man-slaying Achilles, and the brutal realities of war and its aftermath he actually engraves there, revealing a world where rape and murder are axiomatic and no one weeps because another weeps. 'Woods' opens with an etymological reduction ('Sylvan meant savage in those primal woods') which initiates a brief history of murder and atrocity. 'Mountains' turns at once to what they signify to Caesars on the march; 'Lakes' speaks of a Christendom 'scarred by torture' and modern foreign ministers holding their councils and conferences by lake shores; 'Islands' recalls pirate lairs, state prisons, Napoleon and Tiberius (on nearby Elba and Capri respectively); 'Plains' again speaks of 'Caesar with all his They' making his date with history on such flat, battle-worthy expanses; and even 'Streams' cannot avoid calling up the Siege of Paris and the Franco-Prussian War of 1870.

'Woods' sums up the way in which human violence infiltrates the most idyllic landscapes: the 'massacre' of a small ash grove casts a shadow on the Rooseveltian optimistic rhetoric revived by Truman's and Eisenhower's America, signalling that 'This great society is going smash'. The 'vast lives of trees' provide the background for a snapshot at a picnic which reveals 'how short | And lower-ordersy the Gang will look'. The affectionate Americanism of this lacks the venom with which the Old Gang was pilloried in the 1930s, holding out the hope of 'the human race | Retaining enough decency to last'. But there is a sting in the tail. If, punningly, 'late man', the johnny-come-lately on the scene of evolution, does not recognize his responsibilities, he may well soon stew in his own belatedness. Auden's angry 1930s millenarianism has now been translated into ecological chiliasm. But there were many in this period who thought it was not 'this great society' but the poet himself that was 'going smash'.

A FAULTLESS LOVE

The American poet and critic Randall Jarrell, in a series of contemporary reviews, has charted what has become the conventional assessment of the American Auden. An early admirer of Auden's poetry, Jarrell found his doubts began with *Another Time*; *New Year Letter* heralded 'the decline and fall of modernist poetry', of poetry 'experimental, lyric, obscure, violent, irregular, determinedly antagonistic to didacticism, general statement, science, the public'; while *The Age of Anxiety* was virtually 'the worst thing that Auden has written'.[10] His comments on the last sum up a general opinion of the post-war work as

> a rhetoric mill grinding away at the bottom of Limbo...an automaton that keeps making little jokes, little plays on words, little rhetorical engines, as compulsively and unendingly and uneasily as a neurotic washes his hands. A poet has turned into a sack of reflexes. Auden no longer has to struggle against standard tricks, set idiosyncrasies, behavior adjustments aged into obsessive behavior – it is these that write his poems.... Page after page the poem keeps saying: *Remember, the real subject of poetry is words....* Underneath the jokes and fantasies and sermons there is a chaotic, despairing, exhausted confusion....all [the] moral sentiments are solemn, hollow whistles in the dark.[11]

In the 1950s Jarrell qualified this verdict with faint praise: 'There is tiredness and flatness about much of *Nones*, a comfortable frivolity about much of *The Shield of Achilles*, that gives the accuracy and truthfulness and virtuosity of the best poems a lonely, disquieting ring.' Auden's leitmotif now, that 'art is essentially frivolous', is 'a waste of great, the greatest powers; but who wastes powers if he can keep from wasting them?' Whereas in the 1930s he wrote 'some of the strongest, strangest and most original poetry that anyone has written in this century', and remains 'the most professional poet in the world' with 'a matter-of-course mastery behind the elaborate formality, the colloquial matter-of-factness', the whole recent œuvre is the work of one who has 'got tired of the whole affair' of writing – and of himself.[12]

The reasons offered for this alleged decline were many and speculative. Philip Larkin's succinct verdict, 'I think people do get pallid if they change countries. Look at Auden', sums up the standard British reaction more even-handedly than those critics who in 1939–40 had decried Auden's 'defection' as an act of treachery, or who later gloated over his 'decline' as punishment for this act of insubordination. More recent speculation has suggested that his mother's death and increasing distress at Kallman's extensive and programmatic promiscuity had led Auden to this pass. Certainly, one of his worst poems in what is generally regarded as his weakest volume, *Homage to Clio* (1960), 'There Will Be No Peace', which he confessed was 'about paranoia',[13] speaks of 'The darkness blotting out hope'. In the same year he wrote elsewhere that 'Providentially – for the occupational disease of poets is frivolity – I was forced to know in person what it is like to feel the prey of demonic forces ... stripped of self control and self respect, acting like a ham actor in a Strindberg play',[14] in recollection of that episode in 1941 when he had almost murdered Kallman in jealous rage.[15]

'Frivolity' recalls Jarrell's censures, and another poem in the collection, 'Merax & Mullin', echoes Jarrell's critique of inflated writing by

> those who would unwish themselves
> Yet blow a trumpet,
> To fill their voids of insufficiency
> With pejorative noises.

Significantly, they have 'cuckolded fingers', and the poem ends with Laodicean (i.e. half-hearted) lovers egged on to swear undying love. The prose text at the centre of the volume, 'Dichtung und Wahrheit' (Poetry and Truth), identified as 'An Unwritten Poem', puzzles over the impossibility of writing a poem which is both artful and true, which can express exactly what is meant by the words 'I love you', without falsifying for artistic effect. Raising the question of sincerity and truthfulness versus artifice and fabrication, history versus story, the meditation embarrasses with its artfully artless parading of what it clearly hints at as a raw and inexpressible private fixation.

The masterly title poem of this understated volume addresses the theme more fruitfully, speaking of Clio as the 'Muse of the unique | Historical fact', 'to whom we turn | When we have lost control... after | We have been found out'. Other poems explore such poetic betrayals of Clio as Virgil's imperialist sycophancy ('Secondary Epic') or her reciprocal fickleness towards the 'Makers of History' or a Tamburlaine reduced like Napoleon and Hitler to his initials and finally to a crossword clue anagram in 'T the Great'. More resolute both aesthetically and emotionally are the dry Brechtian conclusion of 'First Things First', 'Thousands have lived without love, not one without water', and the Frostian apophthegms of 'The More Loving One', observing of the stars that 'for all they care, I can go to hell', and noting that on earth indifference is the least one fears.

There is certainly some falling-off in this volume, which could charitably be attributed to the miseries of a far from faultless love. In 1947 Auden had confided to Alan Ansen: 'I've come to the conclusion that it's wrong to be queer.... the reasons why are comparatively simple. In the first place, all homosexual acts are acts of envy. In the second, the more you're involved with someone, the more trouble arises, and affection shouldn't result in that.'[16] This seems to have become a settled conviction: in 1969 he wrote in his essay on his BBC friend Joe Ackerley, 'Few, if any, homosexuals can honestly boast that their sex-life has been happy' (FA 451).

In his 1964 Introduction to *The Protestant Mystics*, Auden sought to moderate the Vision of Eros (rooted too deeply in the Vision of Dame Kind – nature, the body – to 'long survive if the parties enter into an actual sexual relation'), with a Vision of

Agape which commands 'love one's neighbour as oneself' and might lead in time to a Vision of God.[17] The transit to a theology of fault redeemed by a faultless divine love necessitated some rewriting of Auden's past as well as of several major poems. 'Spain' and 'September 1, 1939' (with its dream of 'universal love') were dropped entirely from the 1966 *Collected Shorter Poems*. The 1933 poem now christened 'A Summer Night' was cut and revised to convert its original middle-class political guilt into that very first vision of Agape of which he gives a sanitized account in 'The Protestant Mystics'.

Allan Rodway has concluded of Auden's homosexuality, 'early acknowledged... never... disturbed... and never abandoned' (despite several heterosexual episodes, including a prolonged and serious affair in the late 1940s with the American Rhoda Jaffe), that 'Its influence on his work, were it not known of, would be literarily imperceptible; known, it is negligible.'[18] I think this is incorrect. Leaving aside the blow-by-blow rhapsodic pornography of *The Platonic Blow* (1948)[19], which is a special case, and the overtly gay poems published posthumously, there are poems such as 'Lay your sleeping head' which certainly gain an erotic plangency if they are read as gender-specific, while others such as 'The Love Feast', 'Dame Kind' and 'A Shock' clearly deploy as key tonal elements the registers of homosexual camp, Firbankian pastiche and theatrical self-mockery (often, interestingly, in consort with an ironically spilt religiosity).

Auden gave some grounds for Rodway's position, in a 1964 introduction which applies his theology of Visions to 'Shakespeare's Sonnets'.[20] There he wrote superciliously of 'The homosexual reader... determined to secure our Top-Bard as a patron saint of the Homintern... uncritically enthusiastic' about the 'Lovely Boy' sonnets, who prefers to ignore the 'unequivocally sexual' Dark Lady sequence 'and the fact that Shakespeare was a married man and a father' (FA 99). Auden's belief that love poetry should have universal appeal does not, however, imply the corollary he assumes here, that its subjects, objects and addressees should therefore be genderless. What happens to a specifically homosexual impulse in his poetry is revealed in the assertion that

> we are confronted in the sonnets by a mystery rather than an aberration... evidenced for me by the fact that men and women

whose sexual tastes are perfectly normal, but who enjoy and understand poetry, have always been able to read them as expressions of what they understand by the word *love*, without finding the masculine pronoun an obstacle. (*FA* 99–100)

Rationalizing his own struggles to reconcile his and Kallman's separate promiscuities with the sentimental–pastoral–comical–romantic domesticity of his last volumes, Auden relies heavily on 'mystery'. All particular loves are now seen to aspire beyond the 'creaturely glory' of Dame Kind, through the visions of Eros and Agape, to the deferred prospect of that final 'mystery', divine love. With biographical hindsight, one can see that the claim that 'the *primary* experience . . . out of which the sonnets to the friend spring was a mystical one' is a transparently personal projection on to a Shakespeare 'to all intents and purposes, anonymous' of Auden's own 'agonized struggle . . . to preserve the glory of the vision he had been granted in a relationship, lasting at least three years, with a person who seemed intent by his actions upon covering the vision with dirt' (*FA* 103). Likewise, his thumbnail-sketch of the Lovely Boy corresponds closely to the most jaundiced of his assessments of Kallman:

a young man who was not really very nice, very conscious of his good looks, able to switch on the charm at any moment, but essentially frivolous, cold-hearted, and self-centered, aware, probably, that he had some power over Shakespeare – if he thought about it at all, no doubt he gave it a cynical explanation – but with no conception of the intensity of feelings he had, unwittingly, aroused. (*FA* 103)

He may affirm of the Vision of Eros 'I do not think it makes any sense to apply to it terms like heterosexual or homosexual', terms which are relevant only to the 'profane erotic experiences' of lust and (a sly dig at heterosexual norms) 'a happy marriage'. But, *pace* Rodway, it is precisely the homosexual configuration of Auden's earthly loves which allows them to be arranged into that vision of a faultless divine Love figured by the Incarnation and Crucifixion.

In 'The Protestant Mystics' he writes of Agape embodied in the vision of Pentecost (*FA* 69), a vision he seeks to celebrate explicitly in such late poems as 'Whitsunday in Kirchstetten'. But it had already been fully explored in that major meditation on Good Friday, 'Horae Canonicae', developed from the opening and title poems of *Nones* to become the concluding section of *The Shield of Achilles*. The poem's spatialized time, diurnal and sempiternal, represented by the three-hour divisions of the Church's day, counterbalances the historicized space of the opening 'Bucolics'. Here, as in subsequent poems, the profane 'love that dare not speak its name' is transfigured into a sacred one embodying the holy and unspeakable name of God.

ALONE WITH OUR FEAT

The vehicle for this undoubtedly blasphemous transfiguration is the account of the Falstaff/Prince Hal relationship in a 1959 essay in *Encounter* offering Auden's extended reflections on Shakespeare's *Henry IV*.[21] Here Auden again cites the 'Lovely Boy' sonnets, with obvious autobiographical charge ('critics who write about Shakespeare', he begins 'reveal more about themselves than about Shakespeare'). Something tragic, he says, lies 'behind all the fun' of Falstaff's absolute devotion to the Prince, a love Falstaff believes returned, though the audience can see he is 'living in a fool's paradise'. Seeking to explain why Falstaff so affects us, Auden offers a parabolic interpretation of *Henry IV* in which, 'Overtly, Falstaff is a lord of Misrule; parabolically, he is a comic symbol for the supernatural order of charity as contrasted with the temporal order of Justice'.

Once granted this licence, Auden can invert all the play's moral absolutes, so that 'What, overtly, is dishonesty becomes, parabolically, a sign for a lack of pride, humility which acknowledges its unimportance and dependence upon others'; while 'What in the real world is promiscuous lust, the treatment of other persons as objects of sexual greed, becomes in the comic world of play a symbol for the charity that loves all neighbors without distinction.' Thus: 'As parable, both the idleness and the drinking, the surrender to immediacy and the refusal to accept reality, become signs for the Unworldly Man as contrasted with Prince Hal who represents worldliness at its best.'

Projecting, one hopes unconsciously, his own self-image from the poem 'The More Loving One', Auden speaks of a Christian God who 'creates a world which he continues to love although it refuses to love him in return'. Such a God appears in the world not as an immortal in human disguise like the Greek gods, 'but as a real man who openly claims to be God', with the inevitable consequence that 'The highest religious and temporal authorities condemn Him as a blasphemer and a Lord of Misrule, as a Bad Companion for mankind.' He appears, that is, as Falstaff, with whom Auden has already identified his own case, as one of 'nostalgia for the state of innocent self-importance' in which a drinker's belly is 'the physical expression of a psychological wish to withdraw from sexual competition and . . . become emotionally self-sufficient'. The essay ends on a confirmatory note of disenchantment: 'history has not as yet provided us with any evidence that the Prince of this world has changed his character.'

In 'Sext', the third poem in 'Horae Canonicae', the 'Prince of this world' presides over all human culture. Just as, without the 'mystery' of the various crafts, we would still be like the social insects, 'slaves of Dame Kind, lacking | all notion of a city', so without the general, the public prosecutor and the hangman that culture (basilicas, divas, dictionaries, pastoral verse alike) could not exist. In the same way, without the perfect blankness of the crowd we could not proclaim that 'all men are our brothers'. But without all these we would also lack the agents, authority and audience for the fraternal murder of Crucifixion about to occur.

In 'Prime', the opening poem of the sequence, the self at the very moment of waking had been like a newborn child without name or history, before it resumed its 'historical share of care | For a lying self-made city' still free of responsibility for time, and therefore 'wholly in the right', 'unvexed', 'intact', an 'Adam sinless . . . still previous to any act'. In 'Nones', however, the Crucifixion is accomplished, and each member of the crowd has woken from the collective trance to grasp (and to deny) his or her individual responsibility for 'This mutilated flesh, our victim'. Now, for each of them, 'we are left alone with our feat'.

The line recalls, gratingly, the end of 'Spain': 'We are left alone with our day.' Then, when the time was short and history to the defeated might say alas but could neither help nor pardon, such collective solitude urged 'conscious acceptance of guilt in the necessary murder' which was still in the future. Now, that murder has always-already occurred, a 'feat' which nothing can expunge. Under all our misrepresentations and self-deceits 'its meaning | Waits for our lives', 'Behind the rapture on the spiral stair', a Vision of Eros which recalls Eliot, and 'under the mock chase and mock capture' of sex, a Vision of Dame Kind which recalls Kallman.

That personal strain returns in the penultimate poem, 'Compline', with its prayer 'in the name of a love | Whose name one's forgotten' for a love whose name he dare not speak, offering only the initials: '*libera* | *Me, libera* C (dear C) | And all poor s-o-b's who never | Do anything properly'. (A late poem, 'Loneliness', finally allows him his proper name as 'Chester, my chum', but significantly, recalling some of the role-reversals of Hal and Falstaff, only as a kind of *deus absconditus* whose anticipated return will banish the 'Gate-crashing ghost' of the title.) The sequence does not, however, end with 'Compline'. Translating via the Hal/Falstaff relation an intense personal distress into a radical theology, Auden at the same time makes both personal and theological narratives the models for a political and social vision.

In many ways this reruns, with a revived spiritual aura, that account of the Fall into knowledge described in 'Sonnets from China', which cast original sin as the foundation of all human culture. 'The Fallen City' supplies the connection here also, stressing the key concern in *Henry IV* that 'unless there is some impersonal principle in which, when the present ruler dies, the choice of his successor can be decided, there will be a risk of civil war in every generation'.[22] Hal, as the essay demonstrates, establishes his credentials as Prince of this world precisely by the ease with which he sacrifices Falstaff, in an 'immolation' which for Auden clearly has intense personal resonance but which, in the context of the play, is necessary for the preservation of civic order.

'Vespers', the sequence's only prose poem, explores the disenchanted recognition that utopian and arcadian visions are 'different fibs' offering no workable models of social organization. The poem puts an essentially secular inflexion on a vision which elsewhere is, on the one hand, sacred and, on the other, profane, drawing from the Crucifixion the reluctant conclusion that 'without a cement of blood (it must be human, it must be innocent) no secular wall will safely stand'. Arcadias, utopias, 'our dear old bag of a democracy', are alike founded on the 'one Sin Offering', in which the victim ritually atones for those fratricidal acts in which human culture originates, whether the Old Testament pastoralist Abel, slain by his tool-making brother Cain, or the pagan Remus, killed by his brother Romulus at the foundation of Rome. ('Dame Kind' in *Homage to Clio* connects the shedding of the 'first innocent blood' in worship of an earth goddess with the emergence of the human from 'a chinned mammal that hard times | had turned carnivore'.)

For this reason, after the heat and dust of the day, the concluding 'Lauds' offers a cool, pre-dawn vision of Agape, neighbourly love, as the real consequence of Good Friday, a salvation from our civic crimes in which 'Men of their neighbours become sensible', able to pray to God to bless the Realm, the People, and 'this green world temporal: | *In solitude, for company.*' What Auden has worked through in this remark-able sequence, in fact, is the true meaning of that phrase from 'September 1, 1939' now dismissed from his canon as incurably dishonest: 'We must love one another or die.'[23]

5

Going Home

HOME TO LUNCH

In the 1958 poem which concludes the main text of *Homage to Clio*, Auden bade 'Good-bye to the Mezzogiorno' and 'those | Who call it home' with the wistful observation that 'though one cannot always | Remember exactly why one has been happy, | There is no forgetting that one was' – which makes the poem appear as much a valediction to happiness as to middle Italy. His new location was to be that ancestral 'gothic North' with which the poem opened.

One would think from the title of his next volume *About the House* (1965), and from its major opening sequence, 'Thanksgiving for a Habitat', which is *about* every room in his converted Lower Austrian farmhouse, that Auden had finally found a settled happiness pottering 'about the house'. Home, and feeling at home, are certainly key themes of the later volumes; but the hesitation of 'those who call it home' indicates the provisionality Auden felt in any dwelling place. The new book's concluding poem, 'Whitsunday in Kirchstetten', speaks of his pleasure at having 'come home | to lunch on my own land', in the only property he ever owned. But even here he sees himself as a 'metic' (a resident alien), whose Anglo-American idiom and Anglican worship set him apart from his neighbours.

Krushchev's threat 'We shall bury you' may be 'unlikely', but the idea of supersession is persistent. The customary prayer for the dead in the local (Roman Catholic) church only serves to remind of that approaching 'catastrophe', personal death, he hopes to greet gracefully. As 'Ascension Day, 1964' has already indicated, though Pentecost celebrates the departing Christ's promise to send the gift of tongues and the Holy Ghost as

Comforter, its actuality lies in those 'Formulae of farewell', where 'Absence remains | The factual loss it is'.

The first poems in 'Thanksgiving for a Habitat' begin, not with home comforts, but with images of that long home which has preoccupied thought from the origins of human culture. 'The Birth of Architecture' sees that birth built on the celebration of death, from the first line's gallery-grave (prefiguring references to Hetty Pegler's Tump and Weland's Stithy, both prehistoric burial mounds), to the closing recognition that only self-conscious creatures, aware of death and 'the meaning of *If*', would bother to 'construct | a second nature of tomb and temple'. In puzzling the monuments of the compacted 'prehistoric *Once*' which precedes our own moment of being, we know that we too, like all the dead generations, will shortly merge with that 'same Old Man | under different names' which is the past. The fact that 'It's our turn now | to puzzle the unborn' already concedes our supersession, and points towards the volume's closing fear that it may now be 'the looter's turn' (that is, ours) to suffer the brutalities of history.

The sequence's title poem deploys anthropology to relativize our own burial practices as much as those of the ancients. If nobody now would want to be buried with such customary possessions as cocktail shaker and transistor radio or chaperoned to the underworld by a strangled daily help, the whimsy only emphasizes how odd are our own definitions of normality. Neither a cradle nor a windowless grave but 'a place | I may go both in and out of', this property acquired in his fifties affords the liminal pleasure of thresholds which necessarily prefigure other more final crossings. Unsurprisingly, then, 'The Cave of Making' where he writes his poems finds its antetype in Weland's Stithy, the blacksmith's workshop of legend in reality a grave mound; and the 'Maker' addressed is the recently deceased Louis MacNeice. By the conclusion, however, MacNeice has come not to haunt but to offer 'companionship' and Christian 'comfort', a 'dear Shade' invited to hang about till the cocktail hour, when that shaker you can't take with you is still of use to the living.

Whether in the cellar ('Down There') or the attic ('Up There'), and even in the lavatory of 'The Geography of the House', where each day we 'Leave the dead concerns of | Yesterday behind us', living in the present means acknowledging that day in the future when we join the 'prehistoric *Once*' ostensibly dismissed at the start of the sequence. Even the sensual indulgences of bathroom and bedroom speak of mortality, each a transitional resting-place prefiguring the last one. 'Encomium Balnae' laments all those dead cultures without hot baths; while 'The Cave of Nakedness' recalls our 'infantile entrance | at... mother's bidding' to whatever bed, and destiny, we are born to. Both bath and bed arouse thoughts of 'disband[ing] from the world'; waking's return, as the poem puts it, to 'the County of Consideration' echoes MacNeice's frontier-crossing to death's 'Country of Unconcern'.

It is no surprise, then, to find that place of maximum bodily indulgence, the kitchen, visited in 'Grub First, Then Ethics' by the shade of Plato. Amidst present pleasures the poem remains aware of all those occasions, from prehistoric hearthstone to this 'all-electric room | where ghosts would feel uneasy', when Plato's *anthropos* gathered round the site of cooking; and it ends by speculating on the hour of his own death (after a good dinner, he hopes). Even the dinner hour itself, 'Tonight at Seven-thirty', only just holds the dead at bay, as ghostly generations of the hearth since before the last Glaciation gather round the meal, and the poet cannot refrain from thinking about Doomsday's last suppers.

Though the first words of the final poem in the sequence, 'The Common Life', dedicated to Kallman, foreground the living room of personal encounters, it too ends with that ogre who 'will come in any case', and wonders in its course that neither of them has been (no casual word, this) 'butchered by accident', or like so many 'silently vanished into | History's criminal noise'. Coming home to lunch or dinner (and to the cocktail hour) is one of the comforts of age for the late Auden, and the chef figures as an improbable culture hero in several poems. But there is usually some spectre at the feast, even if it sits below the salt.

Addressing Kallman in 'The Common Life', he sees the living room equally as a place not of residence but transit:

> the catholic area you
> (Thou, rather) and I may enter
> without knocking, leave without a bow.

81

The decor is 'a secular faith' that requires each visitor to compare its 'dogmas' with his own before deciding if 'he would like to see more of us'. The verbal playfulness of those dancing pronouns should alert us to the influence exerted by words such as 'secular faith' and 'dogma' on the non-denominational, lower case of 'catholic' and 'protestant'. This lower-case levelling likewise reflects back on the eccentric capitalization of pronouns:

> There's no *We* at an instant,
> only *Thou* and *I*, two regions
> of protestant being which nowhere overlap.

The capitalized English 'I' seems somehow to downgrade the other pronouns, particularly 'you'. Capitalizing 'Thou', then, is intended to restore a proper equality. But, whereas in most European languages the second person singular is an intimate, familiar form, appropriate to the relationship of lovers or what this poem calls 'cater-cousins', its obsolescence in Standard English renders its anachronistic usage here oddly formal, bestowing on Kallman a reverence normally reserved for God.

Auden reflects on the significance of pronouns in such essays as 'The I Without a Self' and 'Balaam and His Ass', but the allusion here recalls the theology of human intersubjectivity of the Viennese Martin Buber, like Kallman neither upper-case 'Catholic' nor 'Protestant' but a Jew who in the Hitler years himself almost vanished into history's criminal noise, and whose most famous book, *Ich und Du* (1923), contests the utilitarian philosophies which reduce experiencing *subjects* to behaving *objects*. 'The Protestant Mystics', indebted to Buber, provides a useful gloss:

> In our relation to one another as intelligent beings...We is not the collective singular We of tradition, but a plural signalling a You-and-I united by a common love for the truth. In relation to each other, we are protestants; in relation to the truth we are catholics. (*FA* 51)

The wider political significance is indicated by remarks in 'Greatness Finding Itself' on 'the grisly success of various totalitarian movements' (including Hitler's), based on misrepresenting the relations between the protestant 'I am' of the individual and the collective 'We are' of catholicism (*FA* 87).

The change of heart in which Auden turned again to the

religion of his childhood was not, to use the drily whimsical phrase of 'Lakes', 'ever so comfy'. It may be 'cosier thinking of night | As more an Old People's Home | Than a shed for a faultless machine' ('A Walk After Dark'); but, taken seriously, Auden's renovated Christianity could be discomfiting and uncomfortable in its claims, and his use of the *New Testament* epithet for the Holy Ghost, the Comforter, often seems euphemistic and placatory (like the Greek use of 'Kindly Ones' for the Furies). The poems regularly and ruefully admit to the shameful struggle between bourgeois ideas of comfyness and the Holy Ghost's demanding sense of 'comfort'. In 'Whitsunday in Kirchstetten', unsettlingly, the elevation of the Host is seen as a ritual in which 'the body of the Second Adam | is shown to some of his torturers' – by which Auden means himself and the rest of the congregation. Similarly, in 'Ascension Day, 1964', the garden birds are comfortable in their ecological niche because they cannot tell 'A hush before storms | From one after massacres': 'Without mixed feelings', they lack the Judas capacity to 'giggle | At any crucifixion'.

'Prologue at Sixty', which concludes *City Without Walls* (1969), reiterates the pleasure in residence. But it also acknowledges, even in the jokey belatedness of its title, the accidental good fortune of being here at all, 'dislodged from elsewhere . . . a Son of the North' from 'outside the limes', the 'unroman lands' beyond the imperial frontier. After ten years he has added 'this unenglish tract' to his 'numinous map' of 'sites made sacred by something read there, | a lunch, a good lay, or sheer lightness of heart'. (The sacerdotal language is significant.) But this place is no more secure, despite its current tranquillity, than any of the others. The lower case of 'unroman' and 'unenglish' suggests just how shallow all territorial claims to possession really are. Motorists on the autobahn peacefully follow a route which since the Stone Age has been used by unwelcome visitors bringing 'violation, | scare and scream, the scathe of battle', Ottoman Turks, Napoleon's armies, or most recently Germans and Russians ('and no joy they brought'). A few kilometres east lie the barbed wire and gun emplacements of the Soviet empire. Not far from here, in the immediate past, 'my day turned out torturers | who read Rilke in their rest periods'.

UNPLACES, UNPERSONS

The Holocaust undermines the ostensible cosiness of this whole volume. 'Joseph Weinheber', the book's keynote poem, acknowledges that 'the Shadow' of recent depravity has not lifted, simply 'moved elsewhere'. Earth has always had her bad patches, 'some unplace with | jobs for torturers'. If 'torturers' points towards the concentration-camp commanders of 'Prologue at Sixty' (guilt distanced and displaced on to others), it also looks back to that disturbing acknowledgement of personal responsibility which had made 'Whitsunday in Kirchstetten' such a day of mixed comfort and despair. Weinheber was a poet too (in Auden's opinion quite a good one), a native of Kirchstetten who would have been Auden's neighbour had he not killed himself on hearing of the German defeat.

The poem does not seek to exculpate Weinheber's Nazi sympathies. 'Prologue at Sixty' acknowledges Auden's own rather remote share in ancestral Viking violence ('Rapacious pirates my people were'). Here, however, he brings the guilt closer to home. In the preface to a revised edition of *The Orators* a year after this poem was written, Auden was to observe that 'my name on the title-page seems a pseudonym for someone else, someone talented but near the border of sanity, who might well, in a year or two, become a Nazi'. He too had once written glibly, in *Spain*, of 'conscious acceptance of guilt in the necessary murder'. No one can cast the first stone. The supposedly decent people we all think we are succumb easily enough, it would seem, to what Auden's friend Hannah Arendt called 'the banality of evil'.[1] Just as the surrounding orchards 'cling to the regime | they know' out of instinctive conservatism, so local bars welcomed the torturers, local girls married them, and what 'Whitsunday' calls 'the *Gemütlichkeit*' (an untranslatable concept embodying homeliness, cosiness and neighbourliness) continued to flourish amidst atrocity.

It is not hard to discern the influence of Arendt's critique on this volume (less than a year later, to her astonishment, Auden actually proposed marriage[2]). Though he finds congenial Weinheber's concern for poetry and the civic good, he does not exonerate him by suggesting it was all a matter of innocently mistaken loyalties. One function of original sin is forgetfulness of our crimes ('Compline' sees this happening with the Crucifixion itself). The peoples who lost the war, already over-eating again, relapse into forgetfulness. Auden's poem, however, insists on remembering: remembering, for example, Franz Jägerstätter, the peasant from a nearby village beheaded by the Nazis for saying 'his lonely Nein to the Aryan state'.

Evil has no favourite suburb: it is, like Auden himself, a metic, cosmopolitan and ultimately stateless. 'Elegy' reports that he acquired a housekeeper because a new ethnic cleansing in 1945 had converted her own Sudeten Germans into 'homeless paupers', as the Czechs 'got their turn to be brutal' (and recalls in the process *About the House*'s 'our turn now'). Since he last came to central Europe, in the 1930s, 'Since' observes, war has 'made ugly | an unaccountable number | of unknown neighbours', who were 'precious as us to themselves'.

The Shadow moves elsewhere, but it never departs. All that the 'Epithalamium' in honour of his niece's marriage can find to celebrate is our stubborn survival as a species, against the odds, wondering

> that life should have got to us
> up through the City's
> destruction layers after
> surviving the inhuman
> Permian purges.

The last phrase slots Europe's recent, murderous history into the geological timescales of an evolution founded in recurrent genocide. Just as the 'red pre-Cambrian light' of 'A Walk After Dark' came to an end with the Cambrian explosion of multicellular life, so the mass extinctions and chance survivals of the Palaeozoic Permian era culminated in the evolution of reptilian life forms, from one of which the ancestor of the first mammals developed. These 'purges', then, were 'inhuman' in a double sense. They were ruthless, amoral and genocidal in a way which recent history has ironically demonstrated to be all too human. But they had nothing to do with us, because we were not even on the scene. The ancestor of all humans, 'the Ur-Papa of princes | and crossing-sweepers', as of the Mudfords, Audens, Seth-Smiths and Bonnergees convened by this wedding, was at the time a mere 'gangrel | Paleocene pseudo-rat' (not even a genuine one) totally unlike its self-important and sometimes equally vicious and equally double-barrelled descendants. Yet the poem remains a genuine celebration, extracting from all this humbling genealogy the idea that each of us as creatures is required to answer to, and take responsibility for the deeds committed in, our own 'Proper Name'.

Auden's last volumes repeatedly speak of human beings as 'creatures', the named, acculturated subject humbled by the reminder of its species-being, defined phylogenetically in 'Prologue at Sixty' as 'a rum creature, in a crisis always, | the anxious species to which I belong'. The poems return, beyond History (made by 'the criminal in us' according to the poem 'Archaeology'), and beyond archaeology too, to the orders of genetics and biology, to that evolutionary defile where, according to 'Unpredictable But Providential', successive catastrophes forced our shrew-ancestor to 'emigrate to un-settled niches', fostering the transformations which led to our ability to 'cogitate about cogitation' | divorcing Form from Matter', but in the process leaving us 'dreading a double death'.

Such long views, placing the species *sub specie aeternitatis*, run the risk of forgiving or at least forgetting what may too easily be redefined as merely local incidents of massacre and genocide. The poems perform a difficult balancing act, scrupulously refusing to forget the chronicle of barbarity which is human history, while celebrating the species' good fortune in avoiding total extinction. The ambivalence is apparent in 'Ode to Terminus', that god of needful boundaries as well as of unhappy endings, which cautiously extols 'the miracle | that we're here to shiver' at all. It is, the poem says, after all remarkable that 'a Thingummy | so addicted to lethal violence' as our universe should somehow have 'secreted a placid | tump with exactly the right ingredients | to start and to cocker Life'. (Auden's quirky language here communicates just the right degree of affec-tionate and eccentric intimacy.) But, undercutting complacency, it reminds us that we are all accountable for the 'manage' (another recurring concept) of the planet 'our colossal immo-desty | has plundered and poisoned'. And, as 'Epistle to a Godson' confides, 'To be responsible for the happiness | of the Universe is not a sinecure'.

This, perhaps, is why *City Without Walls* closes on so belated a

'Prologue'. In the terms of Auden's Christian millenialism, the world is always still to be won, and the human race to be redeemed. The book had begun with a title poem, set in New York, whose first speaker gets carried away in the sleepless early hours with apocalyptic fantasies of a world in terminal decline. The unbounded spaces which were beyond the Pale in olden times are now 'lawless marches', 'Asphalt Lands' and 'wilderness' *within* the City itself, which is now a Megalopolis protected from the 'glare of Nothing' only by the witless noise of its various subcultures. The voice which responds to this gloomy jeremiad casts it as an exercise in literary *Schadenfreude* with lineages in Juvenal and Jeremiah.

A third and final voice interrupts the squabbling pair with a bored, practical demand to get some sleep: it will all look different in the morning. The personal death with which the volume ends is thus pre-emptively figured here as the prologue to the awakening on that day of resurrection and judgement when all shall be called to account for their stewardship. Until that moment, however, the creature lives in a state of endless translation (playing on the etymology of the word as a carrying across frontiers), in which 'the creatured Image' of God is divorced from 'the Likeness', estranged from itself in the perpetually reinstated gaps between signifier, signified, and referent. The reunion of this trinity would be quite literally mortifying, focused in the closing appeal to the 'Giver-of-Life' to 'translate for me | till I accomplish my corpse at last'. On this chilling note book and 'Prologue' end.

ALONE WITH OUR FEET

The play on words which speaks of accomplishing a corpse indicates Auden's sense of the paradoxical nature of mortality. Completion is extinction. Mind and body are mortal, but they are made of immortal matter, temporarily held together by a mutual friend, for, as he observed in an unpublished fragment, 'Man has not two separate natures but is an indivisible trinity of Mind, Body, and Person.'[3]

This is the theme of 'No, Plato, No' in the last, posthumous collection, *Thank You, Fog* (1974), which begins by rejecting the

Platonic wish for abstract, disembodied being. He cannot imagine, he says, anything he would less like to be than 'a disincarnate Spirit', unable to chew, sip, touch surfaces, breathe summer scents, or hear speech and music and 'gaze at what lies beyond' ('gaze' emphasizing the physicality of the act as 'beyond' loiters ambiguously between physical and metaphysical). His ductless glands and other bodily organs might, however, justifiably resent the person in possession, and it could well be that his Flesh wants him to die so that it can be free to become 'irresponsible matter'.

Auden here rejects the traditional Christian–Platonic dualism of soul and body. From his earliest writings, however, he had discerned a profounder dichotomy between irresponsible carnal being and responsible consciousness, reconciled in the 'Person' (as the Third Person of the Trinity mediates Father and Son). He had attempted to theorize this in his curious casting of Falstaff, 'the fellow with the great belly', as the 'comic symbol for the supernatural order of Charity' (*DH* 207, 198). That, perhaps, is why the thresholds of waking and sleep provide the liminal experience of so many poems, for it is here that one mode of being slips quietly over the frontier into the other. A comment in a 1943 essay called 'Purely Subjective' explains this transitional state as Auden's most representative 'immediate religious experience' (explored as such in the opening poem of 'Horae Canonicae'):

> I wake into my existence to find myself and the world that is not myself already there, and simultaneously feel responsible for my discovery. I can and must ask 'Who am I? Do I want to be? Who do I want and who ought I to become?' I am, in fact, an anxious subject.[4]

As, with age, the gap widened between Auden's ideal self-image and his actual cumbrous body and ravaged face, the anxiety of the subject intensified. The final poem of *Epistle to a Godson*, 'Talking to Myself', addresses the bodily self as a capitalized 'You', a 'strange rustic object' which 'I, made in God's Image but already warped' has to bow down to as 'Me'. (The parody of the doctrine of the Trinity is playfully apparent here.) This body becomes, then, another site of the self's displacement, 'my mortal manor, the carnal territory | allotted to my manage, my fosterling too', which he must earn money to support, and without whose 'neural instructions' his conscious self could do or know nothing. No self-respecting person could accept science's conviction that the birth of this unique self was a mere random event, responding instead in Falstaffian tones: 'Random my bottom! A true miracle, say I, | for who is not certain that he was meant to be?' It was Falstaff who, challenged that 'Thou art not what thou seem'st', first duplicitously asserted 'I am not a double man' (1 Henry IV, v. iv. 102–end). This hitherto unremarked source for the American title of New Year Letter provides an important link, via the Shakespeare criticism, between Auden's early materialism and the 'worldly Christianity'[5] of his later years.

'Encomium Balnae' had described a locked bathroom as the only place where a self can be really self-possessed and, 'self-important | as an only child', without embarrassment 'present a Lieder Abend | to a captive audience of his toes'. It is the facticity, the undeniable givenness, of the body (Georg Groddeck's 'It', Freud's Id) which makes it both humbling and comforting to the self-conscious Person, reminding it of its double host, as Auden had written years before in 'Letter to Lord Byron':

> I can't think what my It had on It's mind,
> To give me flat feet and a big behind.

This fallen archness strolls in carpet-slippers through all the last volumes. Left alone with his feet in a steaming bath or, fondling the 'almost feminine flesh' of old age in the solitary bed of 'A Lullaby', imagining himself 'sinless and all-sufficient' in the den of himself, the later Auden returns again and again to the strange interplay between what the latter poem calls 'the verbalising I' and 'the belly-mind... down below the diaphragm, | the domain of the Mothers'.

The body has become modish in recent years, largely as a result of the influence of Foucault on the academy. But the Foucauldian body is characteristically one in extremis, tortured, mutilated, dismembered, flayed, or dying romantically of fashionable diseases. The body is a major theme of Auden's last volumes; but this is a much less glamorous body, as a whole sequence of poems in Epistle to a Godson reminds us, its ectoderm inhabited, as 'A New Year Greeting' says, by yeasts, bacteria and viruses, capable of erupting into acne, athlete's foot or a boil;

overweight, with a beer belly, subject to the minor ailments which, says 'Lines to Dr Walter Birk', 'the organs of old men | suffer in silence'. Among such ailments 'Ode to the Diencephalon' in *Thank You, Fog* lists 'goose-flesh, the palpitations, the squitters' and a capitalized 'ACUTE LUMBAGO', discomforts as unprepossessing and unpoetic as the corresponding comforts are middle class and unheroic.

This body, the lavatorial humour of 'The Geography of the House' had already warned, can 'Keep us in our station... When we get pound-noteish', ensuring that we are 'taken short' (in the crudest physical sense) just as we are about to engage in 'Higher Thought'. But it has its own heroisms, as can be seen in a 1939 review which suggests the link between the (in his own way) heroic survivor Falstaff and the heroic suicide Ernst Toller:

> [T]he Liberal *Aufklärung* was wrong: in the last analysis we *are* lived, for the night brings forth the day, the unconscious IT fashions the conscious fore-brain; the historical epoch grows the idea; the subject matter creates the technique – but it does so precisely in order that it may itself escape the bonds of the determined and the natural. The daemon creates Jacob the prudent Ego, not for the latter to lead, in self-isolation and contempt, a frozen attic life of its own, but to be a loving and reverent antagonist; for it is only through that wrestling bout of which the sex act and the mystical union are the typical symbols that the future is born, that Jacob acquires the power and the will to live, and the demon is transformed into an angel.[6]

Probably the single most important statement of a belief which encompasses all Auden's thinking about the human condition, early and late, 'Jacob and the Angel' translates Old Testament tale into sacred truth, mythos into a materialist theology which speaks of the limits and conditions of being human, in art, history, religion and personal life alike. Thirty years later, 'Moon Landing', addressing a human achievement which had been 'merely a matter | of time' from the moment our hominid ancestors flaked the first flint, used the occasion to reflect on a duality and disproportion in which 'our selves, like Adam's, | still don't fit us exactly, modern | only in this – our lack of decorum'. 'Our apparatniks will continue making | the usual squalid mess called History,' he says. But the real human achievement is to have created a world of sense and conscience 'where to die has a meaning'.

BUGGERING OFF

Auden's first three post-war volumes all ended with praise or prayer lauding the living, sociable world of human intercourse, taking their cue from the command of the penultimate poem of *Nones*, 'Precious Five', to 'Bless what there is for being'. Indeed, the idea of blessing is almost as prevalent in the post-war volumes as 'love' was in the pre-war ones. But from *About the House* onwards, though the blessing continues, each volume ends by contemplating that bodily death which disperses the human trinity. 'Talking to Myself' had admitted to being 'scared of our divorce', but nevertheless urged the body to

> Remember, when *Le bon Dieu* says to You *Leave him!*,
> please, please, for His sake and mine, pay no attention
> to my piteous *Don'ts*, but bugger off quickly.

Though there is no thought of suicide, the wish for a quick and easy death is the grace note of *Thank You, Fog*, summed up in the last poem he wrote, a haiku wishing for the good Lord to take him. The title poem encapsulates these mixed feelings, fusing the reasonable wish of age to feel 'cosy' and at home in 'specific places', the friendly fog cutting him off with friends in the English countryside over Christmas, with the Browning-esque premonition of death as a fog in the throat, the isolation of 'this special interim' a metonymy for one's entire earthly stay, soon to be discontinued.

In one of the last pieces he wrote, placed by his editor at the close of what Auden probably knew would be his final volume, he returns to the agenda set by 'Precious Five'. 'The Entertainment of the Senses' is, appropriately, an antimasque written in September 1973 in collaboration with Kallman, setting the seal on the various libretti which they had co-authored over the previous three decades. In the end, this is what the whole 'anxious subject' called Wystan Hugh Auden had been about: the entertainment of the senses, in a double sense. If his senses had entertained, performed for, his own appreciative audience, he too had entertained, given a stage to, put up with them. The sequence is full of punning wordplay. Touch, for example, urges us not to be touchy or lose touch, warning 'There's no sex-life in the grave', a word which ends every section of the piece. As the personified Death of his earliest, disowned play enters unseen, the antimasque, in a last act of textual second thoughts, emends the desperate wishful optimism of 'September 1, 1939' with a gallows humour that insists ' "We must love one another *and* die!" ' The text's closing couplet converts current vogue word into a final irony:

> The moral is, as they have said:
> Be with-it, with-it, with-it till you're dead.

With-it, that is, until one is without, crossing the frontier into that final elsewhere beyond all sense.

Some time in the early hours of Saturday, 29 September 1973, in a small hotel on the Walfischgasse, just round the corner from the Vienna State Opera, an anxious subject impatient to be gone buggered off quickly. The autopsy diagnosed a heart attack. Little more than a year later, Chester, fourteen years his junior, so restless and unfaithful in life, died of the same. The inconstant ones had finally come home.

Notes

CHAPTER 1. WE ARE LIVED BY POWERS

1. Edward Mendelson (ed.), Preface to W. H. Auden, *Selected Poems* (London: Faber & Faber, 1979), p. ix.
2. Samuel Hynes coined the title in his monumental *The Auden Generation: Literature and Politics in England in the 1930s* (London: Bodley Head, 1976). For revisionist readings of the 1930s, see the essays in John Lucas (ed.), *The 1930s: A Challenge to Orthodoxy* (Sussex: Harvester Press, 1978), Jon Clark *et al.* (eds.), *Culture and Crisis in Britain in the Thirties* (London: Lawrence & Wishart, 1979), Frank Gloversmith (ed.), *Class, Culture and Social Change: A New View of the 1930s* (Sussex: Harvester Press, 1980); and Adrian Caesar, *Dividing Lines: Poetry, Class and Ideology in the 1930s* (Manchester: Manchester University Press, 1991). For general histories, see A. T. Tolley, *The Poetry of the Thirties* (London: Gollancz, 1975), and Valentine Cunningham, *British Writers of the Thirties* (Oxford: Oxford University Press, 1989).
3. In Clifton Fadiman (ed.), *I Believe* (London: Allen & Unwin, 1939); repr. in *EA* 372–80, all quotations at 373.
4. Introduction, in W. H. Auden (ed.), *The Portable Greek Reader* (New York: Viking Press, 1948), 3–38, at 9–10, 37–8; repr. in *FA* 3–32, at 10, 32.
5. Cited in Dennis Davison, *W. H. Auden* (London: Evans Bros, 1970), 226.
6. In Geoffrey Grigson (ed.), *The Arts To-day* (London: Bodley Head, 1935), 1–21, at 19; repr. in *EA* 332–42, at 341.
7. 'Honour', in Graham Greene (ed.), *The Old School: Essays by Diverse Hands* (London: Cape, 1934) 9–20; repr. as 'The Liberal Fascist', *EA* 321–7, at 321–2.
8. 'A Literary Transference', *Southern Review* (Summer 1940), 83.
9. Nevill Coghill, in R. March and Tambimuttu (eds.). *T. S. Eliot: A Symposium* (London: Editions Poetry, 1948), 82.
10. 'The Poet of the Encirclement', *New Republic* (Oct. 1943); repr. in *FA* 351–7, at 351–2.

11. Dorothy J. Farnan, *Auden in Love* (London: Faber & Faber, 1985), 65–6.
12. 'A Letter of Introduction', in G. Handley-Taylor and T. D'Arch Smith (eds.), *C. Day-Lewis, The Poet Laureate, A Bibliography* (London: St James Press, 1968), p. v.

CHAPTER 2. ON THE FRONTIER

1. *EA* provides checklists for these volumes (Appendix III, 431–3). Titles in the following paragraphs are those given in *Collected Poems* (1976).
2. W. H. Auden, *For the Time Being* (London: Faber & Faber, 1945), 37.
3. 'As it seemed to us', *The New Yorker* (3 Apr. 1965), 180.
4. Stella Musulin, 'Auden in Kirchstetten', in Katherine Bucknell and Nicholas Jenkins (eds.), *'In Solitude, For Company': W. H. Auden after 1940* (Auden Studies 3; Oxford: Oxford University Press, 1995), 222–3.
5. Humphrey Carpenter, *W. H. Auden: A Biography* (London: Allen & Unwin, 1981), 98–101.
6. Geoffrey Grigson (ed.), *The Arts To-day* (London: Bodley Head), 17; *EA* 340.
7. Introduction, in W. H. Auden (ed.), *The Portable Greek Reader* (New York: Viking Press, 1948), 33; *FA* 28.
8. Ibid. 38; *FA* 32.
9. W. H. Auden and T. C. Worsley, *Education Today – and Tomorrow* (London: Hogarth Press, 1939); *EA* 380–6, at 384.
10. *The Criterion* (Apr., 1930); *EA* 301–2.
11. Edward Mendelson, *Early Auden* (London: Faber & Faber, 1981), 23.
12. R. H. S. Crossman (ed.), *Oxford and the Groups* (Oxford: Basil Blackwell, 1934), 89–101, at 98.
13. *The Twentieth Century* (Sept. 1932); repr. in Michael Roberts (ed.), *New Country* (London: Hogarth Press, 1933), 209–13. On this, see the Symposium in Katherine Bucknell and Nicholas Jenkins (eds.), *W. H. Auden: 'The Map of All My Youth'* (Auden Studies 1; Oxford: Oxford University Press, 1990), 173–95.
14. Louis MacNeice, 'Poetry To-Day', in Geoffrey Grigson (ed.), *The Arts To-day* (London: Bodley Head, 1935), 23–67, at 57.
15. Grigson (ed.), *The Arts To-day*, 17.
16. Preface, Michael Roberts (ed.), *New Signatures: Poems by Several Hands* (London: Hogarth Press, 1932); repr. in Frederick Grubb (ed.), *Michael Roberts: Selected Poems and Prose* (Manchester: Carcanet Press, 1980), 63–9, at 68–9.

CHAPTER 3. TRUTH IS ELSEWHERE

1. George Orwell, *Inside the Whale* (London: Gollancz, 1940), 36–7.
2. Edward Mendelson, *Early Auden* (London: Faber & Faber, 1981), 206.
3. W. H. Auden, *New Year Letter* (London: Faber & Faber, 1941), 119.
4. Humphrey Carpenter, *W. H. Auden: A Biography* (London: Allen & Unwin, 1981), 288–97; John Haffenden (ed.), *W. H. Auden: The Critical Heritage* (London: Routledge & Kegan Paul, 1983), 33–40.
5. Charles Osborne, *W. H. Auden: The Life of a Poet* (London: Macmillan, 1982), 206–7.
6. Haffenden (ed.), *W. H. Auden*, 299.
7. Introduction, *The Faber Book of Modern American Verse* (London: Faber & Faber, 1956), 9–21, at 14–15; repr. in *DH* 354–68, at 359–60.
8. W. H. Auden, in Edward Mendelson (ed.), *The Prolific and the Devourer* (New York: Ecco Press, 1994), 21.
9. Auden, *The Faber Book of Modern American Verse*, 19; *DH* 367.
10. 'The Poet of the Encirclement', *New Republic* (Oct. 1943); *FA* 351.
11. W. H. Auden, 'Introduction', *A Choice of de la Mare's Verse* (London: Faber & Faber, 1963); repr. in *FA* 384–94, at 385.
12. 'A Preface to Kierkegaard', in *New Republic* (May 1944), 683–6, at 683.
13. Reinhold Niebuhr, *The Nature and Destiny of Man* (New York: Charles Scribner's Sons, 1941–3), i (1941), 194–6. Auden's review appeared as 'The Means of Grace', *New Republic* (June 1941), 765–6. On Auden's relations with the Niebuhrs, see Ursula Niebuhr, 'Memories of the 1940s', in Stephen Spender (ed.), *W. H. Auden: A Tribute* (London: Weidenfeld & Nicolson, 1974), 104–18.

CHAPTER 4. THE INCONSTANT ONES

1. Letter to E. R. Dodds, *Missing Persons: An Autobiography* (Oxford: Oxford University Press, 1977), 136.
2. Richard Crossman's collection, *The God that Failed: Six Studies in Communism* (London: Hamish Hamilton, 1950), was widely interpreted, on both left and right, as a recantation of 1930s left-wing beliefs. The contributors, who included Auden's friend Spender, his hero André Gide, fellow tenant the black novelist Richard Wright, and Koestler, a former Comintern agent he had met in Spain, appear in retrospect to be trying to salvage some independent left position from which the 1930s and the Cold War had hijacked them. The book contains much that illuminates Auden's own feelings at the time.

3. Reinhold Niebuhr, *The Irony of American History* (New York: Charles Scribner's Sons, 1962), 155. The Preface is dated January 1952.

4. 'Our Italy', *Griffin* (Apr. 1952), 3.

5. C. Wright Mills, *The New Men of Power* (New York: Harcourt Brace, 1948).

6. W. H. Auden, Introduction to *The Complete Poems of Cavafy* trans. Rae Dalven (London: Hogarth Press, 1961); repr. in *FA* 333–44).

7. See Eric Hobsbawm, *Age of Extremes: The Short Twentieth Century 1914–1991* (London: Michael Joseph, 1994), 238.

8. Charles Osborne, *W. H. Auden: The Life of a Poet* (London: Macmillan, 1982), 235–7.

9. *Partisan Review* (Apr. 1950), 390–4.

10. Collected in Randall Jarrell, *Kipling, Auden & Co: Essays and Reviews 1935–1964* (New York: Farrar, Straus & Giroux, 1980), 55–6.

11. Ibid. 145–6.

12. Ibid. 229–30.

13. Monroe K. Spears, *The Poetry of W. H. Auden: The Disenchanted Island* (New York: Oxford University Press, 1963), 327.

14. The Dean of New York (ed.), *Modern Canterbury Pilgrims: The Story of 23 Converts and why they chose the Anglican Communion* (Oxford: A. R. Mowbray, 1956), 32–43, at 41.

15. See Dorothy J. Farnan, *Auden in Love* (London: Faber & Faber, 1985), 53–66. Richard Davenport-Hines (*Auden* (London: Heinemann, 1995), 294–5) attributes what Auden called the 'very unpleasant dark-night-of-the-soul experience' recorded here to the enmity aroused by his appointment to the Oxford Professorship of Poetry in 1956. It is likely that Auden's contentious re-entry to British (specifically Oxford) circles, together with some more recent betrayal by Kallman, reawakened that earlier trauma, at a time when his mother had just died and he felt doubly abandoned in an alien country.

16. Alan Ansen, *The Table Talk of W. H. Auden*, ed. Nicholas Jenkins (London: Faber & Faber, 1991), 80.

17. W. H. Auden, Introduction to Anne Freemantle (ed.), *The Protestant Mystics* (London: Weidenfeld & Nicolson, 1964); repr. in *FA* 49–78, at 69–70.

18. Allan Rodway, *A Preface to Auden* (London: Longman, 1984), 18. On Jaffe, see Farnan, *Auden in Love*, 119–28.

19. Privately printed by (*inter alia*) the spoof publisher 'The Gobble Grope Press' (New York, 1948).

20. W. H. Auden, Introduction to Shakespeare's *Sonnets*, ed. William Burto (New York: New American Library, 1964); repr. in *FA* 88–108.

21. 'The Fallen City: Some Reflections on Shakespeare's "Henry IV"', *Encounter* (Nov. 1959), 21–31; repr. with minor changes, and an

added bitterness in the title, as 'The Prince's Dog', in *DH* 182–208. Quotations in the next two paragraphs at 21, 25, 27, 29–31, 26, 31 (*DH* 182, 191, 198, 203–4, 207–8, 195–6, 208).
22. Ibid. 23 (*DH* 188).
23. Foreword to B. C. Bloomfield and Edward Mendelson, *W. H. Auden: A Bibliography 1924–1969* (Charlottesville, Va.: University Press of Virginia, 1972), p. viii. On the history of Auden's phrase, see John Fuller, *A Reader's Guide to W. H. Auden* (London: Thames & Hudson, 1970), 260.

CHAPTER 5. GOING HOME

1. Hannah Arendt, *Eichmann in Jerusalem: A Report on the Banality of Evil* (New York: Viking Press, 1963).
2. See Carol Brightman (ed.), *Between Friends: The Correspondence of Hannah Arendt and Mary McCarthy 1949–1975* (London: Secker & Warburg, 1995), 269–72; and Elizabeth Young-Bruehl, *Hannah Arendt* (New Haven: Yale University Press, 1982), 455.
3. Quoted in Nicholas Jenkins, 'Some Letters from Auden to James and Tania Stern', in Katherine Bucknell and Nicholas Jenkins (eds.), *'In Solitude, For Company': W. H. Auden after 1940* (Auden Studies 3; Oxford: Oxford University Press, 1995), 51.
4. *Chimera* (Summer 1943), 3.
5. 'The Fall of Rome' (unpublished essay for *Life Magazine*, 1966), in Bucknell and Jenkins (eds.), *'In Solitude, For Company'*, 133.
6. *New Republic* (Dec. 1939), 293.

Select Bibliography

WORKS BY W. H. AUDEN

(Except where otherwise indicated, Auden's work is published by Faber & Faber, London, and Random House, New York.)

Collections
Collected Shorter Poems 1927–1957 (1966).
Collected Longer Poems (1968).
Collected Poems, ed. Edward Mendelson (1976; new edn., 1991). (Publishes only those poems Auden approved.)
Selected Poems, ed. Edward Mendelson (1979). (Includes poems Auden suppressed.)
The English Auden: Poems, Essays and Dramatic Writings, 1927–1939, ed. Edward Mendelson, 1977. (Includes uncollected and subsequently suppressed writings.)
The Dyer's Hand and Other Essays (1963; New York: 1962; new edn., 1975).
Forewords and Afterwords ed. Edward Mendelson (1973; new edn., 1979). (Previously uncollected prose.)
Plays and Other Dramatic Writings, 1928–1938 (with Christopher Isherwood), ed. Edward Mendelson (1989; Princeton, NJ: Princeton University Press, 1988).
Libretti and Other Dramatic Writings 1939–1973 (with Chester Kallman), ed. Edward Mendelson (1993; Princeton, NJ: Princeton University Press).
Juvenilia: Poems 1922–1928, ed. Katherine Bucknell (1994; Princeton, NJ: Princeton University Press).

Main Separate Volumes
(Excluding libretti, small press publications, and edited works.)

Poems (1928; privately printed by Stephen Spender).
Poems (1930; rev. edn. 1933, with omissions and seven new poems).

The Orators: An English Study (1932; rev. 2nd edn. 1934; 3rd edn. 1966).

The Dance of Death (1933).

The Dog Beneath the Skin or Where is Francis? (with Christopher Isherwood) (1935).

The Ascent of F6 (1936).

Look, Stranger! (1936; as *On This Island* (New York: 1937)).

Spain (1937).

Letters from Iceland (with Louis MacNeice) (1937).

On the Frontier (with Christopher Isherwood) (1938).

Journey to a War (with Christopher Isherwood) (1939; rev. edn. 1973).

Another Time (1940).

New Year Letter (1940; as *The Double Man* (New York: 1941)).

For the Time Being (1945; New York, 1944).

The Age of Anxiety (1948; New York, 1947).

The Enchafèd Flood or The Romantic Iconography of the Sea (Charlottesville, Va.: University Press of Virginia, 1950).

Nones (1952; New York, 1951).

The Shield of Achilles (1955).

Homage to Clio (1960).

About the House (1966; New York: 1965).

Secondary Worlds (The Eliot Memorial Lectures, 1968; New York: 1969).

City Without Walls (1969; New York: 1970).

Academic Graffiti (1971).

A Certain World: A Commonplace Book (1971; New York: Viking Press, 1970).

Epistle to a Godson (1972).

Thank You, Fog (1974).

The Prolific and the Devourer, ed. Edward Mendelson (New York: Ecco Press, 1994).

BIOGRAPHICAL AND BIBLIOGRAPHICAL STUDIES

Beach, Joseph Warren, *The Making of the Auden Canon* (Minneapolis: University of Minnesota Press, 1957). (Included here for its massive deconstruction of Auden's rewritings and suppressions.)

Bloomfield, B. C., and Mendelson, Edward, *W. H. Auden: A Bibliography 1924–1969* (2nd edn.; Charlottesville, Va.: University Press of Virginia, 1972).

Spender, Stephen, (ed.), *W. H. Auden: A Tribute* (London: Weidenfeld & Nicolson, 1975).

Gingerich, Martin E., *W. H. Auden: A Reference Guide* (London: George Prior, 1977).

Mendelson, Edward, *Early Auden* (London: Faber & Faber, 1981). (Much more than a biography, but placed here because it uses a biographical narrative to effect a major critical reinterpretation of Auden's work in the 1930s.)

Carpenter, Humphrey, *W. H. Auden: A Biography* (London: Allen & Unwin, 1981). (Immensely thorough and comprehensive account of the life.)

Osborne, Charles, *W. H. Auden: The Life of a Poet* (London: Macmillan, 1982). (Readable and lively approach to the life.)

Miller, Charles H., *Auden: An American Friendship* (New York: Charles Scribner's Sons, 1983).

Haffenden, John (ed.), *W. H. Auden: The Critical Heritage* (London: Routledge & Kegan Paul, 1983). (Reprints the major reviews of the separate volumes as they appeared.)

Rodway, Allan, *A Preface to Auden* (London: Longman, 1984). (Combines biography and critical interpretation.)

Farnan, Dorothy J., *Auden in Love* (London: Faber & Faber, 1985.) (Much on the relationship with Kallman, by Kallman's father's second wife.)

Ansen, Alan, *The Table Talk of W. H. Auden*, ed. Nicholas Jenkins (London: Faber & Faber, 1991).

Clark, Thekla, *Wystan and Chester* (London: Faber & Faber, 1995).

Davenport-Hines, Rupert, *Auden* (London: Heinemann, 1995). (An excellent new critical biography, with much new material.)

CRITICAL STUDIES

Scarfe, Francis, *Auden and After: The Liberation of Poetry 1930–1941* (London: George Routledge & Sons, 1942).

Hoggart, Richard, *Auden: An Introductory Essay* (London: Chatto & Windus, 1951).

—— *W. H. Auden* (London: Longmans, Green & Co, for The British Council, 1957).

Everett, Barbara, *Auden* (Edinburgh: Oliver & Boyd, 1964).

Spears, Monroe K., *The Poetry of W. H. Auden: The Disenchanted Island* (New York: Oxford University Press, 1963).

—— (ed.), *Auden: A Collection of Critical Essays* (Englewood Cliffs, NJ: Prentice-Hall, 1964).

Blair, John G., *The Poetic Art of W. H. Auden* (Princeton, NJ: Princeton University Press, 1965).

Greenberg, Herbert, *Quest for the Necessary: W. H. Auden and the Dilemma of Divided Consciousness* (Cambridge, Mass: Harvard University Press, 1968).

Replogle, Justin, *Auden's Poetry* (London: Methuen, 1969).

Nelson, Gerald, *Changes of Heart* (Berkeley and Los Angeles: University of California Press, 1969).

Fuller, John, *A Reader's Guide to W. H. Auden* (London: Thames & Hudson, 1970).

Davison, Dennis, *W. H. Auden* (London: Evans Bros, 1970).

Bahlke, George W., *The Later Auden* (New Brunswick: Rutgers University Press, 1970).

—— (ed.), *Critical Essays on W. H. Auden* (New York: Prentice Hall, 1991).

Duchêne, François, *The Case of the Helmeted Airman* (London: Chatto & Windus, 1972).

Johnson, Richard, *Man's Place: An Essay on Auden* (Ithaca, NY: Cornell University Press, 1973).

Buell, Frederick, *W. H. Auden as a Social Poet* (Ithaca, NY: Cornell University Press, 1973).

Callan, Edward, *Auden: A Carnival of Intellect* (Oxford: Oxford University Press, 1983).

McDiarmid, Lucy, *Saving Civilization: Yeats, Eliot, and Auden between the Wars* (Cambridge: Cambridge University Press, 1984).

—— *Auden's Apologies for Poetry* (Princeton, NJ: Princeton University Press, 1990).

Carter, Ronald (ed.), *Thirties Poets: 'The Auden Group'* (London: Macmillan, 1984).

Smith, Stan, *W. H. Auden* (Oxford: Blackwell, 1985).

—— *(ed.)*, *Auden* Special Number, *Critical Survey*, 6/3 (Oxford: Oxford University Press, 1994).

Bold, Alan (ed.), *W. H. Auden: The Far Interior* (London: Vision Press, 1985).

O'Neill, Michael, and Gareth Reeves, *Auden, MacNeice, Spender: The Thirties Poetry* (London: Macmillan, 1992).

Hecht, Anthony, *The Hidden Law: The Poetry of W. H. Auden* (Cambridge, Mass.: Harvard University Press, 1993).

Much recent Auden scholarship and criticism has appeared in the three volumes of Auden Studies so far published by Oxford: Oxford University Press, edited by Katherine Bucknell and Nicholas Jenkins:

W. H. Auden, 'The Map of All My Youth': Early Works, Friends and Influences (1990).

W. H. Auden: 'The Language of Learning and the Language of Love': Uncollected Writings: New Interpretations (1994).

'In Solitude. For Company': W. H. Auden after 1940 (1995).

The W. H. Auden Society also issues an irregular *Newsletter*.

Index

*Recent and
Forthcoming Titles
in the
New Series of*

WRITERS AND
THEIR WORK

WRITERS AND THEIR WORK

RECENT & FORTHCOMING TITLES

Title	Author
W.H. Auden	*Stan Smith*
Aphra Behn	*Sue Wiseman*
A. S. Byatt	*Richard Todd*
Lord Byron	*J. Drummond Bone*
Angela Carter	*Lorna Sage*
Geoffrey Chaucer	*Steve Ellis*
Children's Literature	*Kimberley Reynolds*
Caryl Churchill	*Elaine Aston*
John Clare	*John Lucas*
Joseph Conrad	*Cedric Watts*
John Donne	*Stevie Davies*
Henry Fielding	*Jenny Uglow*
Elizabeth Gaskell	*Kate Flint*
William Golding	*Kevin McCarron*
Graham Greene	*Peter Mudford*
Hamlet	*Ann Thompson & Neil Taylor*
Thomas Hardy	*Peter Widdowson*
David Hare	*Jeremy Ridgman*
Tony Harrison	*Joe Kelleher*
William Hazlitt	*J.B. Priestley; R.L. Brett (introduction by Michael Foot)*
Seamus Heaney	*Andrew Murphy*
George Herbert	*T.S. Eliot (introduction by Peter Porter)*
Henry James - The Later Writing	*Barbara Hardy*
James Joyce	*Steven Connor*
King Lear	*Terence Hawkes*
Philip Larkin	*Laurence Lerner*
Doris Lessing	*Elizabeth Maslen*
David Lodge	*Bernard Bergonzi*
Christopher Marlowe	*Thomas Healy*
Andrew Marvell	*Annabel Patterson*
Ian McEwan	*Kiernan Ryan*
A Midsummer Night's Dream	*Helen Hackett*
Walter Pater	*Laurel Brake*
Brian Patten	*Linda Cookson*
Jean Rhys	*Helen Carr*
Richard II	*Margaret Healy*
Dorothy Richardson	*Carol Watts*
Romeo and Juliet	*Sasha Roberts*
The Sensation Novel	*Lyn Pykett*
Edmund Spenser	*Colin Burrow*
J.R.R. Tolkien	*Charles Moseley*
Leo Tolstoy	*John Bayley*
Angus Wilson	*Peter Conradi*
Virginia Woolf	*Laura Marcus*
Charlotte Yonge	*Alethea Hayter*

TITLES IN PREPARATION

Title	Author
Peter Ackroyd	*Susana Onega*
Kingsley Amis	*Richard Bradford*
Antony and Cleopatra	*Ken Parker*
Jane Austen	*Robert Clark*
Alan Ayckbourn	*Michael Holt*
J. G. Ballard	*Michel Delville*
Samuel Beckett	*Keir Elam*
William Blake	*John Beer*
Elizabeth Bowen	*Maud Ellmann*
Emily Brontë	*Stevie Davies*
S.T. Coleridge	*Stephen Bygrave*
Crime Fiction	*Martin Priestman*
Daniel Defoe	*Jim Rigney*
Charles Dickens	*Rod Mengham*
Carol Ann Duffy	*Deryn Rees Jones*
George Eliot	*Josephine McDonagh*
E.M. Forster	*Nicholas Royle*
Brian Friel	*Geraldine Higgins*
Henry IV	*Peter Bogdanov*
Henrik Ibsen	*Sally Ledger*
Kazuo Ishiguro	*Cynthia Wong*
Julius Caesar	*Mary Hamer*
Franz Kafka	*Michael Wood*
John Keats	*Kelvin Everest*
Rudyard Kipling	*Jan Montefiore*
Langland: *Piers Plowman*	*Claire Marshall*
D.H. Lawrence	*Linda Ruth Williams*
Measure for Measure	*Kate Chedgzoy*
William Morris	*Anne Janowitz*
Vladimir Nabokov	*Neil Cornwell*
Sylvia Plath	*Elizabeth Bronfen*
Alexander Pope	*Pat Rogers*
Dennis Potter	*Derek Paget*
Lord Rochester	*Peter Porter*
Christina Rossetti	*Kathryn Burlinson*
Salman Rushdie	*Damian Grant*
Sir Walter Scott	*John Sutherland*
Mary Shelley	*Catherine Sharrock*
P. B. Shelley	*Paul Hamilton*
Stevie Smith	*Alison Light*
Wole Soyinka	*Mpalive Msiska*
Laurence Sterne	*Manfred Pfister*
Jonathan Swift	*Claude Rawson*
The Tempest	*Gordon McMullan*
Dylan Thomas	*Graham Holderness*
Derek Walcott	*Stewart Brown*
Evelyn Waugh	*Malcolm Bradbury*
John Webster	*Thomas Sorge*
Mary Wollstonecraft	*Jane Moore*
William Wordsworth	*Nicholas Roe*
Working Class Fiction	*Ian Haywood*
W.B. Yeats	*Ed Larrissy*

JOHN·CLARE
John Lucas

Setting out to recover Clare – whose work was demeaned and damaged by the forces of the literary establishment – as a great poet, John Lucas offers the reader the chance to see the life and work of John Clare, the 'peasant poet' from a new angle. His unique and detailed study portrays a knowing, articulate and radical poet and thinker writing as much out of a tradition of song as of poetry. This is a comprehensive and detailed account of the man and the artist which conveys a strong sense of the writer's social and historical context.

"Clare's unique greatness is asserted and proved in John Lucas's brilliant, sometimes moving, discourse." **Times Educational Supplement.**

John Lucas has written many books on nineteenth- and twentieth-century literature, and is himself a talented poet. He is Professor of English at Loughborough University.

0 7463 0729 2 paperback 96pp

GEORGE HERBERT
T.S. Eliot
With a new introductory essay by **Peter Porter**

Another valuable reissue from the original series, this important study – one of T. S. Eliot's last critical works – examines the writings of George Herbert, considered by Eliot to be one of the loveliest and most profound of English poets. The new essay by well-known poet and critic Peter Porter reassesses Eliot's study, as well as providing a new perspective on Herbert's work. Together, these critical analyses make an invaluable contribution to the available literature on this major English poet.

0 7463 0746 2 paperback 80pp £5.99

CHILDREN'S LITERATURE
Kimberley Reynolds

Children's literature has changed dramatically in the last hundred years and this book identifies and analyses the dominant genres which have evolved during this period. Drawing on a wide range of critical and cultural theories, Kimberley Reynolds looks at children's private reading, examines the relationship between the child reader and the adult writer, and draws some interesting conclusions about children's literature as a forum for shaping the next generation and as a safe place for developing writers' private fantasies.

"The book manages to cover a surprising amount of ground . . . without ever seeming perfunctory. It is a very useful book in an area where a short pithy introduction like this is badly needed." **Times Educational Supplement**

Kimberley Reynolds lectures in English and Women's Studies at Roehampton Institute, where she also runs the Children's Literature Research Unit.

0 7463 0728 4 paperback 112pp

LEO TOLSTOY
John Bayley

Leo Tolstoy's writing remains as lively, as fascinating, and as absorbing as ever and continues to have a profound influence on imaginative writing. This original and elegant study serves as an introduction to Tolstoy, concentrating on his two greatest novels – *War and Peace* and *Anna Karenina* – and the ancillary texts and tales that relate to them. By examining how Tolstoy created a uniquely spacious and complex fictional world, John Bayley provides a fascinating analysis of the novels, explaining why they continue to delight and inform readers today.

John Bayley is Warton Professor of English Emeritus at St Catherine's College, University of Oxford.

0 7463 0744 6 paperback 96pp

EDMUND SPENSER
Colin Burrow

Considered by many to be the greatest Elizabethan poet, Edmund Spenser's writing has inspired both admiration and bewilderment. The grace of Spenser's language and his skilful and enchanting evocation of the fairy world have, for many, been offset by the sheer bulk and complexity of his work. Colin Burrow's considered and highly readable account provides a reading of Spenser which clarifies the genres and conventions used by the writer. Burrow explores the poet's taste for archaism and allegory, his dual attraction to images of vital rebirth and mortal frailty, and his often conflictual relationship with his Queen and with the Irish landscape in which he spent his mature years.

Colin Burrow is Fellow, Tutor and College Lecturer in English at Gonville & Caius College, University of Cambridge.

0 7463 0750 0 paperback 128pp

HENRY FIELDING
Jenny Uglow

In this fresh introduction to his work, Uglow looks at Fielding in his own historical context and in the light of recent critical debates. She identifies and clarifies many of Fielding's central ideas, such as those of judgement, benevolence and mercy which became themes in his novels. Looking not only at the novels, but also at Fielding's drama, essays, journalism and political writings, Uglow traces the author's development, clarifies his ideas on his craft, and provides a fascinating insight into eighteenth-century politics and society.

Jenny Uglow is a critic and publisher.

0 7463 0751 9 paperback 96pp

HENRY JAMES
The Later Writing
Barbara Hardy

Barbara Hardy focuses on Henry James's later works, dating from 1900 to 1916. Offering new readings of the major novels and a re-evaluation of the criticism to date, she considers language and theme in a number of Jamesian works, including *The Ambassadors, The Wings of the Dove* and *The Golden Bowl,* and engages with his autobiographical and travel writing and literary criticism. Hardy's analysis traces two dominant themes – the social construction of character and the nature of creative imagination – and reveals James to be a disturbing analyst of inner life.

Barbara Hardy is Professor Emeritus at Birkbeck College, University of London.

0 7463 0748 9 paperback 96pp

DAVID LODGE
Bernard Bergonzi

Internationally celebrated as both a novelist and a literary critic, David Lodge is one of Britain's most successful and influential living writers. He has been instrumental in introducing and explaining modern literary theory to British readers while maintaining, in regard to his own work, "faith in the future of realistic fiction". Bergonzi's up-to-date and comprehensive study covers both Lodge's critical writing as well as his novels of the past 35 years (from *The Picturegoers* to *Therapy*) and explores how he expresses and convincingly combines metafiction, realism, theology and dazzling comedy.

Bernard Bergonzi is Emeritus Professor of English at the University of Warwick.

0 7463 0755 1 paperback 80pp

DAVID HARE
Jeremy Ridgman

David Hare is one of the most prolific, challenging, and culturally acclaimed playwrights in Britain today. Jeremy Ridgman's study focuses on the dramatic method that drives the complex moral and political narratives of Hare's work. He considers its relationship to its staging and performance, looking in particular at the dramatist's collaborations with director, designer, and performer. Hare's writing for the theatre since 1970 is set alongside his work for television and film and his achievements as director and translator, to provide a detailed insight into key areas of his dramatic technique particularly dialogue, narrative, and epic form.

Jeremy Ridgman is Senior Lecturer in the Department of Drama and Theatre Studies at Roehampton Institute, London

0 7463 0774 8 paperback 96pp